neri & hu design and research office

neri & hu design and research office

with essays by
Rafael Moneo and Sarah M. Whiting

thresholds:
space, time and practice

To Amata, Jack, Connie, George, Jeremiah, Hannah and Zachariah,
for your love and support

First published in the United Kingdom in 2021 by
Thames & Hudson Ltd, 181A High Holborn, London WC1V 7QX

First published in the United States of America in 2021 by
Thames & Hudson Inc., 500 Fifth Avenue, New York, New York 10110

Reprinted 2022

Neri&Hu Design and Research Office – Thresholds: Space, Time and Practice
© 2021 Neri&Hu Design and Research Office
Essay © 2021 Rafael Moneo
Essay © 2021 Sarah M. Whiting

Designed by Neri&Hu Design and Research Office

British Library Cataloguing-in-Publication Data
A catalogue record for this book is available from the British Library

Library of Congress Control Number 2020951866

ISBN 978-0-500-34360-9

Neri&Hu Design and Research Office
Exclusive Edition
ISBN 978-0-500-34379-1

Printed and bound in China by RR Donnelley

Be the first to know about our new releases,
exclusive content and author events by visiting
thamesandhudson.com
thamesandhudsonusa.com
thamesandhudson.com.au

contents

"If you find nothing...there, don't worry, just leap up another flight of stairs"
: Franz Kafka

introduction
lyndon neri and rossana hu

The Chinese words for describing space and time share one common character – *jian* (間), an ideogram composed of a 'sun' between a pair of 'doors'. *Jian* can be roughly translated as a gap, a pause, a space, or the space between two structural parts, and is often used as the counterpart to another character to form a range of meanings. When combined with the character for 'empty', it takes on the meaning of 'space'; combined with the character for 'late' it takes on the meaning of 'night'. Some meanings are abstract and general, such as 'within', 'among' or 'between', while others are more specific, to describe 'room', 'chamber' or 'world'; still others are related to the temporal realm, expressing 'evening' or 'time'. Some people have associated the concept of *jian*, like that of the Japanese word *ma*, with violinist Isaac Stern's description of music as the silence between notes, or evoke it even more poetically as 'an emptiness full of possibilities, like a promise yet to be fulfilled'. While there is no direct English equivalent to *jian*, in an architectural sense this term is often used to describe a threshold condition, or the physical mediation between two contrasting spatial environments, such as interior and exterior, or public and private. This is why we have chosen *Thresholds* as the leading title for this monograph, as it represents where we position ourselves, as mediators traversing and operating between space, time and interdisciplinary practices.

In the years since we published our first monograph in 2017, we have taken pause to reflect on how our practice has grown and evolved. The previous monograph was decisively focused on adaptive reuse projects that contend with the role of history, preservation and how the designer can mediate between past and present. After looking at the collective works of the practice (which span interiors, architecture, product design and graphic design), it was clear that our second monograph could not be neatly consolidated under a single theme if we wanted to do justice to the practice's interdisciplinary exploration. Just as *jian* relies on pairing with other characters to give itself an expansive array of meanings, so we have extended this conceptual framework into multiple thematic categories; many of them have evolved from our early 'obsessions' with voyeurism, historical preservation, interiority and objecthood. This monograph represents an intersection of multiple investigations and recurring themes. Some have matured over the years, while others are recently charted territory, opening up new chapters for our design research in the future.

The monograph is structured into six main categories focused on architecture and interior design, with the last section dedicated to product design. Conceptually, we wanted to bookend the categories with similar themes with very contrasting constraints, such as adaptive reuse versus ground-up architecture. Seen as a spectrum, moving from the topic of 'reflective nostalgia', continuing a dialogue with the first monograph, this second monograph ends with 'future artefact', which is also underpinned by a strong theme of temporal continuity and history. Moving through the monograph, the reader will journey through different issues we face today: adaptive reuse and the role of history; reimagined spatial legibility associated with voyeurism; tectonics and the use of poché; a search for a connection back to the vernacular; the role of collective memory and fragments; and finally the crafting of everyday objects. Most of the works showcased here are projects based in China and the rest of Asia, but we believe many of these issues transcend our immediate geographical confines. We have also chosen to republish some notable works that were featured in our first monograph, augmented with new images, as we feel these older projects are fundamental to understanding our evolving approach to new projects.

As an office, we have been blessed by the generosity of the design patrons, from global corporations to neighbourhood entrepreneurs to individuals, whose vision and zeal have allowed our projects to be realized. We do not take for granted the enormous support of the global design community, whose creative, social and educational agendas connect us to a network of friends and collaborators. They continue to inspire us and push us beyond our boundaries, from educational institutions to cultural and professional establishments, from media platforms to design conferences. Similarly, the colleagues who work alongside us continue to impress with their commitment to rigour and excellence. We cannot thank everyone individually, but a list of recognition in the Collaborators section shows our appreciation for each invaluable individual. We are humbled by Professor Rafael Moneo and Dean Sarah M. Whiting's graciousness for injecting their scholarship and critical reading of our work. We thank Lucas Dietrich and Elain McAlpine of Thames & Hudson for their publishing guidance.

A few years ago, we came upon a curious discovery regarding the evolution of *jian* (間): instead of a 'sun' between 'doors', the earlier ancient ideogram was a 'moon' between 'doors'. This was fascinating, since the transformation from moon to sun did not alter the meaning of the word through time. As we traverse between east and west, architecture and product design, old and new, practice and education, our aim as a practice remains unchanged – to create meaningful experience crossing thresholds and bridging gaps. Whether it is peeking through our doors to see the moonlight or the sunbeam, each project is a new beginning. Each, a new threshold.

clarity, pulchritude and precision
rafael moneo

One of the greatest joys for those who, as in my case, have dedicated a good part of their lives to teaching architecture is to see that those who were their students are now praiseworthy architects. Hence, even though I have always tried to express my opinion only about those works of architecture that I have seen first-hand, I break with the habit by writing some thoughts about the work of Lyndon Neri and Rossana Hu after seeing the published drawings and images of their work.

I was surprised, first of all, by the clarity and precision of their work – virtues that allow them to intervene in existing architectures without distorting them, without interfering with them, but nevertheless suffusing them with new life. It is not a question, therefore, of remodelling the building, but of 'occupying' it with a new architecture that guarantees the continuity of the first building in time, although it lives outside it. Projects such as the Garage (p. 28), the Recontextualization of History (p. 56) and the Vertical Lane House (p. 80) are exemplary in that they show how to act on an existing architecture without transforming its materiality: this becomes a suitable framework for the new building, projected on to the old one without affecting it and maintaining its original integrity, and without confusing both. Rethinking the Split House (p. 140) shows how the procedure has a broader scope than the intervention in a strict building, and that as this becomes the entire city, the structural values of the type of which it is part prevail, alien and indifferent to the linguistic change that our times impose. The literal juxtaposition of two architectures gives rise to a new architectural experience that forces us to consider them together and that is present to us in the sharpness with which the details are executed and in the use of materials.

The details encourage us to speak of precision and pulchritude, be it in the geometric definition of a building's shapes or in the beauty of the execution. Consider the windows of the Vertical Lane House. The windows emphasize the value of the plan, drawing on it as a simple change in texture: rectangles and squares built with treated wood board and with a metal profile are inscribed in the stucco to maintain its strict condition as a geometric figure. The wood assumes the presence of a remote nature in the abstract and immaculate surface of the wall. Unexpectedly, the protection of the window glass, those rectangles and squares of which I spoke, rotates and transforms the perception we had of that wall. The architectural experience of that area takes place around the windows, the cuts made in the façade. The architects' talent lies in not making themselves seen, in staying in the background, making the transforming mechanism imperceptible, giving priority to the phenomenon of seeing a wall, a surface that has breath, which lives.

Let us talk now about the materials. If we were to penetrate the interior of the Lantern (p. 216), we would have to do so through a three-dimensional mesh that appears to us as if it was the materialization of an artificial atmosphere, in which the appearance of architecture is going to take place – an architecture that takes pleasure in showing us the structure of the space in which it is produced by isolating a portion of it.

The meeting and contact between the materials with which it operates – brass, stone, wood, glass – define a space created to seduce and attract all the senses. The materials used are not unrelated to the precision and pulchritude of which we spoke. The attitude that we have seen when working on existing architectures, the juxtaposition I mentioned, can also occur in projects with more ambitious content, such as the Sanctuary (p. 230), the House of Remembrance (p. 184), the Unfolding Village (p. 112) or the Brick Wall (p. 264). But now the juxtaposition is that of cultures. In them, we find diverse cultures in close proximity and still compatible. Asia, with its centuries of architectural tradition, makes itself felt in such projects, but there is also a sense that Neri and Hu want to be present in the discussion about architecture that takes place in the schools where they were educated.

They show a consideration of the past from the perspective we have of the present, as the goal of an agenda from which it will be difficult for architects to escape today. Of all the projects mentioned, the one in which, in my opinion, Neri and Hu have managed to go furthest in what seems to me to be their objectives, is the Brick Wall, for both the rigour of the plan and the carefully crafted details in their use of the material. It is an architecture not alien to Chinese vernacular architecture, but also one in which we recognize interests not so different from those of the courtyard houses of Mies van der Rohe, for example, which naturally remind us of a contemporary version of a remote historical reference in Western culture. The Brick Wall is an exercise in juxtaposition of times and cultures that leads us to think that the future agenda of Neri&Hu will include transcending borders, always a difficult and attractive endeavour, for which the work they have built until now must be seen as a valuable and splendid introductory experience.

Rafael Moneo was born in Tudela, Spain, in 1937, and graduated in 1961 from the Architecture School of Madrid. A professor at the Architecture Schools of Barcelona and Madrid, he was appointed Chairman of the Architecture Department, Harvard University Graduate School of Design, where he is now Emeritus Josep Lluís Sert Professor in Architecture.

Notable among Moneo's works are the National Museum of Roman Art in Mérida, the Kursaal Congress Centre and Auditorium in San Sebastián, the Museums of Modern Art and Architecture in Stockholm, Our Lady of the Angels Cathedral in Los Angeles and the extension to the Prado Museum in Madrid. His book Theoretical Anxiety and Design Strategies in the Work of Eight Contemporary Architects *(2004) has been translated into eight languages.*

Moneo has been a member of the Royal Academy of Fine Arts of Spain since 1997, and elected Honorary Member of the American Academy of Arts and Letters in 2013. He has received numerous awards, including the Pritzker Prize for Architecture in 1996, the Royal Gold Medal of the Royal Institute of British Architects in 2003, the Prince of Asturias Prize in the Arts in 2012, the National Prize for Architecture in 2015 and the Praemium Imperiale by the Japan Art Association in 2017.

doubling down
sarah m. whiting

Four years ago, Lyndon Neri and Rossana Hu published their first monograph, *Neri&Hu Design And Research Office: Works and Projects 2004–2014*, documenting the initial ten years of their eponymous practice and confirming their remarkable talents, particularly in the area of adaptive reuse. Most firms would have subsequently rested on the laurels of such a publication, particularly given the amount of work that the office is currently undertaking, but instead of pausing, Neri&Hu has doubled down on interrogating its own practice, the result of which is this provocative publication.

The idea of 'doubling down' conjures images of a doubled blackjack bet; more broadly, it means becoming more resolute in your position. And indeed, this new volume plumbs positions, mostly by doubling them: *reflective nostalgia*; *nomadic voyeurism*; *inhabitable strata*; *future artefact*. With these doubles, Neri&Hu do not succumb to the easy binaries that all too often render architectural research facile, splitting people, work and even materials into opposing camps, rather than uniting them into shared investigations. Instead, like Hesse, the studio goes beyond such easy pairs to probe new insights: insights into its work, into modernity, into globalization, into China's evolving urbanism and ruralism; and, finally, insights into where architecture might be taking Neri&Hu and all of us as we find our way now well into the twenty-first century.

One such doubling throughout the work collected here seems at first blush to be an incongruous pairing of solidity and surface. The Garage (p. 28) might be the most evident version of this pairing – the original brick factory building is paired with a steel structure supporting a taut white box that slips over one end of the existing structure. The easy opposition of traditional masonry versus modern steel frame, of structural façade versus free façade, is called into question by the grid of punched, deep windows in the white modern box, their steel inner frames recalling, doubling, the steel structure itself. With these windows, we realize that we no longer live in a world of modern versus traditional, but have moved beyond, to a world that feeds new possibilities of materials, of structures and of façades that can carry layers of history while also mediating new interpretations.

In the Recontextualization of History project (p. 56), a similar play of materials calls into question our typical architectural assumptions: the brick interior walls appear thin, in a surprising contrast with the clearly thick structural brick walls of the façade, but the thinnest item of all is the exquisite interior railing, which, like the pendant light structure, introduces the most delightful if incongruous airiness to the most solid of structures – a former police station. With this play of existing and infill, which sometimes makes the existing appear to be infill, Neri&Hu exercises the depth and range of their expertise, which, as this book reveals, extends from graphics to landscape, with extraordinary attention to detail at every gradation in between, whether it be the fabric curtain, or 'lantern', of the Constellation of Enclosures (p. 154), or the stone façade cantilevering overhead of Sculpted Light (p. 194). Every material is considered and carefully detailed, without ever succumbing to the common trap of overarticulating every surface and every joint. In short, Neri&Hu exhibit an all too rare confidence in the ensemble: finesse does not succumb to fussiness; instead, an ensemble or a whole always remains foregrounded.

Wholeness arriving out of a holistic approach: this totality is the beyond, the insight that Lyndon Neri and Rossana Hu offer us in this volume and in their practice – that is, both in their work and in the very practice of their pairing, as the ensemble of Neri&Hu.

Sarah M. Whiting is the Dean and Josep Lluís Sert Professor of Architecture at the Harvard University Graduate School of Design. She is a design principal and co-founder of WW Architecture, and served as the Dean of the School of Architecture at Rice University from 2010 to 2019. Whiting's research is broadly interdisciplinary, with the built environment at its core. An expert in architectural theory and urbanism, she has particular interests in architecture's relationship with politics, economics and society and how the built environment shapes the nature of public life. Whiting is editor of the single-essay book series POINT, has published her own writings in journals ranging from ANY *to* Wired, *as well as in collections including* Shaping the City, Mies in America, Six Authors in Search of an Architect *and* An Architecture for All Senses: The Work of Eileen Gray.

memory is not an instrument for surveying the past but its theatre. it is the medium of past experience, just as the earth is the medium in which dead cities lie buried. he who seeks to approach his own buried past must conduct himself like a man digging. he must not be afraid to return again and again to the same matter; to scatter it as one scatters earth, to turn it over and one turns over soil. for the matter itself is only a deposit, a stratum, which yields only to the most meticulous examination what constitutes the real treasure hidden within the earth.

– walter benjamin, a berlin chronicle (1932)

reflective nostalgia

This first set of projects captures our obsession with reflective nostalgia. Many of our projects are based on the premise that nostalgia, rather than being regressive, offers a productive means to engage with issues of heritage, collective memory, displacement and urban renewal. Whereas restorative nostalgia 'attempts a trans-historical reconstruction of the lost home', reflective nostalgia 'dwells on the ambivalences of human longing and belonging and does not shy away from the contradictions of modernity'.[1] As a genre, these renovation efforts share similar strategies – using material contrast, tectonic differentiation, formal assemblage and surgical grafting. However, each project comes with its own set of unique issues related to how one engages a tumultuous concession-era heritage, resistance to the commercialization of faux historical relics, and the role of representation in the dialectics between past and present. In the works presented, one can sense the delicate balance between the contrasts of new and old, smooth and textured, refined and raw. Many of our projects 'graft' new skins upon existing corpus and bones – this prosthetic approach is evident in the Recontextualization of History project (p. 56), where layers of decay were removed and a new appendage in glass and steel was added to contrast with the existing building.

The surgical nature of these projects also speaks to an archaeological approach of peeling back the layers, working with deletions as much as additions. In the spirit of Gordon Matta-Clark, whose self-described works are about 'making space without building it', they express the techniques of erosion and erasure, calibrated to produce new, unexpected spatial readings. In some cases, floor slabs in corridors are removed to transform hallways into dramatic atriums. In the Vertical Lane House (p. 80), slab cuts were introduced above the restaurant to provide hotel guests with just the slightest glimpse into the communal realm below – these visual slippages happen even for the kitchen, injecting surprising aspects of theatricality into the mundane.

We also weave remnants together by recomposing an assemblage of found fragments to unify the parts. Tectonic legibility is expressed at times with a horizontal datum (plane of reference) or in other instances is explicitly highlighted through material coding. This is most clearly expressed in the Vertical Lane House, where all existing steel structures are painted black, all existing walls left raw and untouched and all new walls finished in white plaster. Ultimately, our aim is not to restore an image of the past or freeze its history, but to create a dialogue between an imagined past and the present moment, such that their coexistence may produce new, subjective readings of history.

100 m (328 ft)

black box redux
number 31

1

shanghai

architectural renovation
interior
products
environmental graphics

More than ten years ago, the practice went through a phase of rapid growth and we relocated to a building in Shanghai's former French Concession. We affectionately named that project, with its painted black façade, the 'black box', liking the implied metaphor of the practice as a crucial recording device of our collective design ideas. This time, with Black Box Redux, we did not merely want to build our new home: the ambition of this project was to build upon the notion of a 'design commune' – an idea initiated more than ten years ago in our Design Republic flagship store – to found a collective creative platform that aspires to bring together the broader design community of Shanghai.

Located within a small complex of ex-industrial buildings in the middle of Shanghai's bustling Jing'an area, the site for our relocation used to be a nondescript four-storey office and dormitory building for the local telecoms company. Instead of discarding it for a new building, we embraced the potential for transformation so the remains would not only survive, but thrive as a creative hub.

Retail, café and staff canteen occupy the ground floor, while our own offices are located above. The existing south staircase stitches all the programmes together, along with a few communal spaces open to the public, which include co-working areas and open kitchen facilities on the first floor, a multi-purpose event space on the mezzanine level between the first and second floors, and a rooftop garden. True to our interdisciplinary intention, we have executed a seamless integration of architecture, interiors, furnishings and graphics.

The first renovation strategy is a reworking of the main façade to completely shift its proportions and reading, without major structural alteration. The repetitive and perfunctory windows of the existing building are partially infilled with glass bricks, while the bottom portions of the new operable windows are strung together with unifying black metal frames, creating the illusion of a series of long horizontal ribbon windows. Glazed green tiles are used to define the rounded staircase that anchors one end of the building and continues across the undulating wall at the base, while a new canopy is added as a welcoming gesture on the street level.

The second strategy is to keep all the existing concrete post-and-beam constructions intact; to celebrate them by leaving them fully exposed. While maintaining the structural grid, a few selective cuts are made into slabs to introduce double-height spaces and a new internal staircase between the second and third floors. The deceptively simple operations of cutting and deleting reveal the layers of spatial potential within a rather ordinary building configuration. In between the existing columns, several steel and ribbed glass enclosures are added, while white box volumes house support spaces. Throughout the project, we intentionally juxtapose these new insertions against the old framework. As a practice, we have been drawn to adaptive reuse opportunities, and this project allows us to celebrate the mundane by reappropriating an artefact of urban excess.

2

3

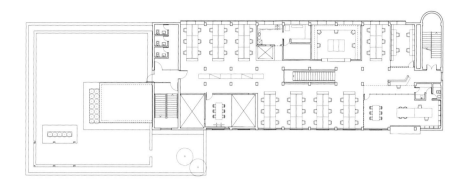

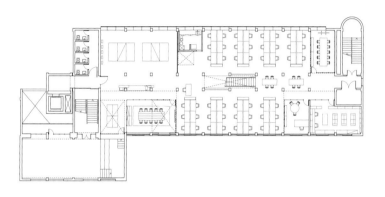

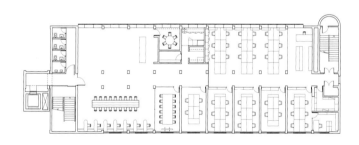

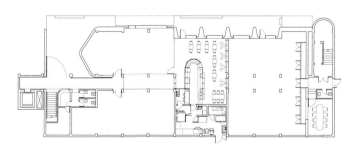

20 m (65½ ft)

4

5

6

7

8

6 lounge and co-working space 7 product lab corridor 8 restroom corridor 9 private office

9

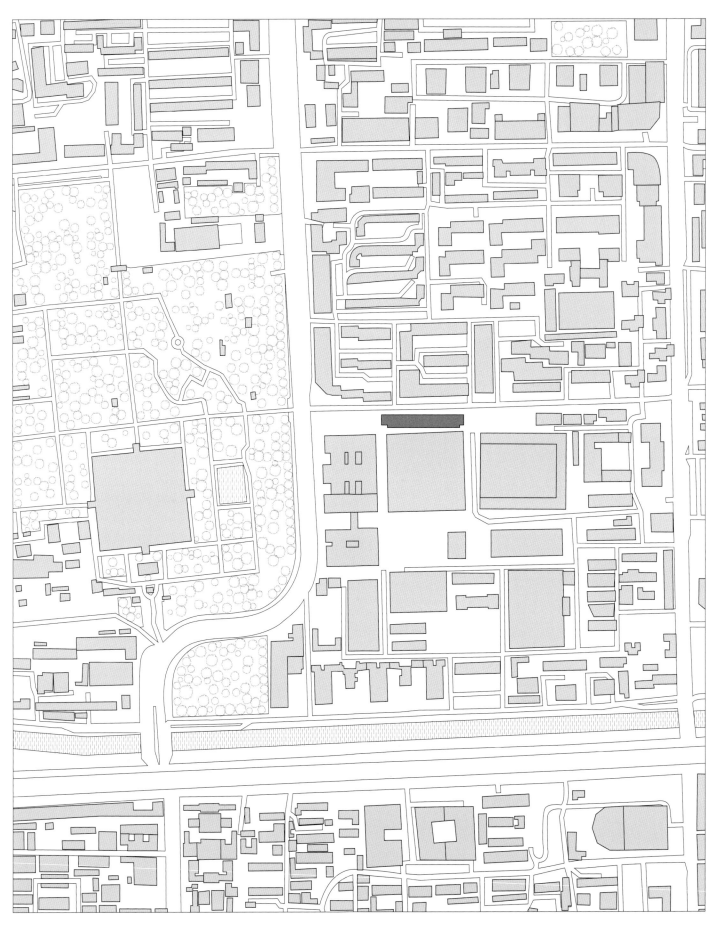

the garage
beijing b+ automobile service centre

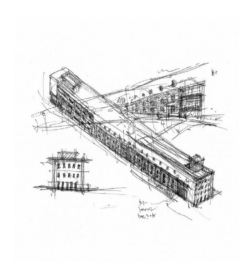

In a city of 26 million inhabitants and 7 million vehicles, being trapped in a car in Beijing's notorious traffic is a compulsory experience. Our approach to the transformation of a former missile-manufacturing factory into an automobile service centre attempts to recapture the allure and magic that was once associated with cars. Along with a café and offices, the project as a whole is conceived as a workshop space. Partly raw and partly refined, it is activated throughout with the energy and spirit of the industrial era.

Architecturally, the original factory has been kept largely intact, with three of its four brick walls remaining untouched. The addition of a new steel-frame structure creates a third level to accommodate the client's capacity needs. Demonstrating a certain tectonic candour, the trio of elements – existing brick building, structural steel frame and inserted white volume – are visually distinct and legible on the façade.

A series of black metal frames redefines the rhythmic window openings, while mirrored glass provides textural intrigue to the mostly monochromatic base. Raw steel-edged glass garage doors at each of the vehicular entries are marked with graphics and signage to guide visitors to distinct areas along the building's nearly 100 m (328 ft) length.

Sitting within the white volume of the building shell at the west end are the main function spaces – office, café and car lift – with each expressed as modularized steel and mesh boxes, a reinterpretation of industrial storage facilities. Mezzanine platforms, stairs and walkways float amid the mysterious black cages, so that cars and people circulate constantly within the space. The pairing of café and automobile workshop combines a surreal juxtaposition of functions, which generate moments of spectacle. Viewing down between the structural beams, peering through the layers of mesh and mirror, there is an allusion to the backstage of a theatrical set, where patrons of the café can steal voyeuristic glimpses of the cars and mechanics.

While the brutality of the materials palette and the unadorned authenticity of the metal assemblage take inspiration from an industrial heritage, an additional layer of textured materials – walnut timber and brushed bronze – provides a sense of hospitality. Custom furniture and lighting pieces adopt the tectonic efficiency of wood-plank and tubular-steel construction, but their material richness and refined detailing also look to the quality of craftsmanship found in antique cars. With this project, we have attempted to break through common expectations of a seemingly utilitarian typology lacking nuance, to inject a sense of warmth into an industrial context and to portray the seductive side of the ubiquitous modern machine.

beijing

architectural renovation
interior
products
branding
environmental graphics

1

2

1 street façade 2 garage entry 3 signage

3

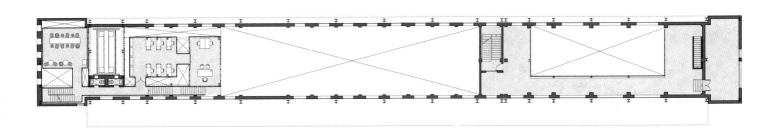

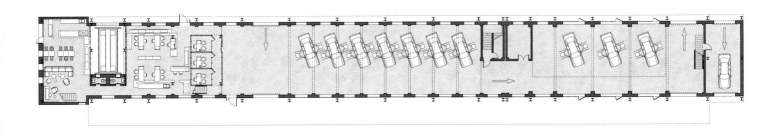

20 m (65½ ft)

4

5

4 café staircase 5 office space

6

7

8

"在人口密聚的城市里，有这样一个宁静的去处，像是上帝的苦心安排"——史铁生

9

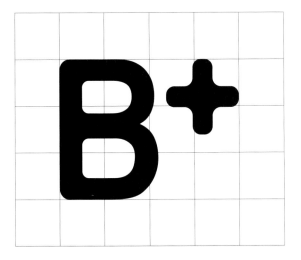

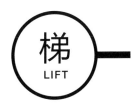

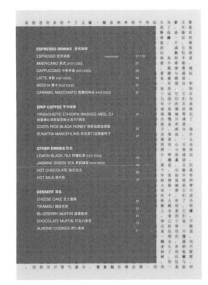

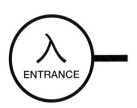

the unifying wall
yuyuan road and together restaurant

Our design for a redevelopment project reconfigured a collection of perfunctory and nondescript office buildings, located on the historic Yuyuan Road in Shanghai, into a mixed-use commercial complex with a sensibility of history, community and conviviality. Situated off a charming sycamore-lined street, the development is an eclectic mixture of ten old and new buildings, each with its own distinct façade. The main design challenge was to define an architectural element that could bring an extent of cohesive harmony and continuity to the site and its existing scattered structures. Drawing inspiration from vernacular Chinese urban architectural typologies, such as the *hutong* neighbourhoods of northern China and the *longtang* alleyways of Shanghai, the wall is a unifying element that brings cohesion, security and a communal feel to a grouping of disparate buildings.

Along the busy street front, the continuity of the wall defines a strong urban edge condition. Breaks in this continuity generate moments of passage and intrigue, creating a gateway to the community within. The wall acts as a filter of views and light, while guiding the visitor through the site. Expanding its role beyond a simple barrier between two spaces, the wall engages with the façades of various buildings, creating dynamic relationships between interior and exterior.

In certain places where existing buildings have formed leftover pockets of unusable area, the wall envelops these areas to create quiet courtyards for the community within. Featuring recycled red bricks, the project elevates a rather common building material through the use of varied brick bonds, including perforated and relief patterns. In contrast, the walls above the brick plane are all painted white to simplify and abstract the discrepancies between the window sizes and the rhythms of different façades.

Deriving the notion of bonding from the unifying wall, we grafted the same spirit into our conceptualization of Together, the flagship restaurant within the complex. Anchoring the corner of the site, the restaurant reinforces its overall ideology of community and sharing with its orientation and open gesture. The formal language of the red-brick wall continues from the exterior into the interior, extending to the central dining area and defining the heart of the restaurant. At just over 200 m^2 (2,150 sq ft), the restaurant spatially and programmatically unites diners with its cosy, relaxed atmosphere within a small footprint. Apart from the primary red-brick language, a second palette of curved, glazed white ceramic tiles and white oak is introduced to the two smaller spaces adjacent to the main dining space to create a sense of domestic tranquillity. Custom-designed brass pendants, classic wicker chairs and ordinary enamel tableware add a layer of convivial refinement that echoes the essence of Together's culinary vision.

shanghai

architectural renovation
interior
products
branding
environmental graphics

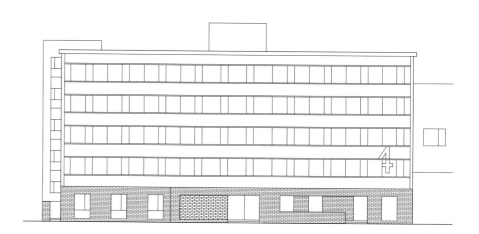

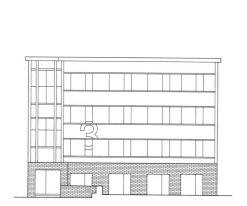

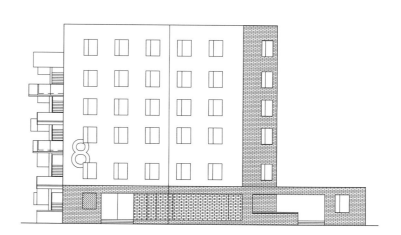

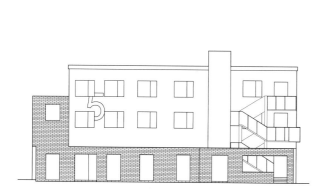

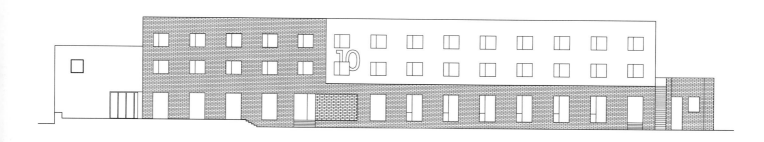

elevations

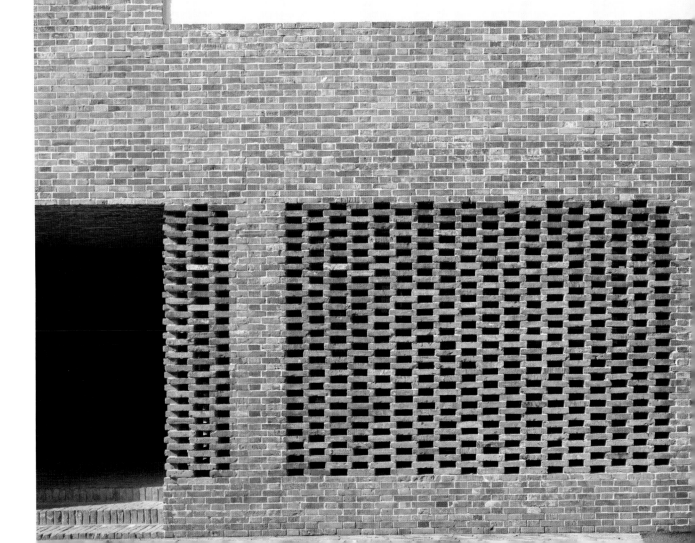

3

4

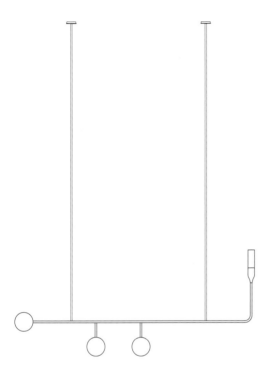

light 1:20

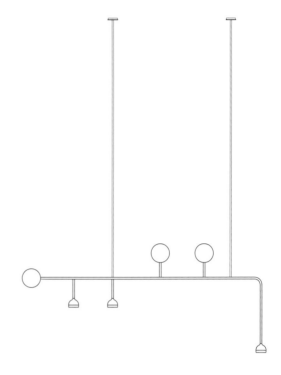

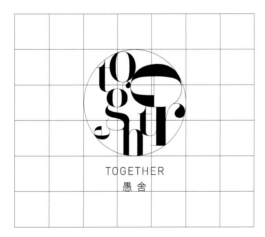

restaurant logo

silkscreened quote

5

6

7

the convenience store
little b retail concept

1

The convenience store has a ubiquitous presence in Asian metropolises. Brightly lit, they shine through the day and night, serving urban inhabitants tirelessly, and Shanghai is no exception. As a new concept store for popular lifestyle brand The Beast, Little B takes the idea of a convenience store to another level. As with any typical convenience store, it offers light food and drink, personal care items and basic home accessories – except that each item here is sourced from various high-end local and international brands, carefully curated for the culturally astute and increasingly discerning taste of Chinese consumers. In thinking about how to embody this new retail concept, our design plays off the perfunctory nature of the modern convenience store and the spontaneity of street culture and 'pop-ups', while carrying out attentive interrogations of materials and curating a rigorous aesthetic that does not cater only to current fads.

Located in Xintiandi, a heavily trafficked commercial area modelled after traditional Shanghai *shikumen* lane houses in the city centre, the storefront respects the classic detailing of the existing architecture, while bringing in fresh elements and materials. The light-grey aggregate concrete found in the original base, lintels and moulding of the building is extended as a canopy above the entry, also forming a base for the window display. To the left of the existing façade, a new addition is clad in curved, white glazed tiles in a vertical pattern, extending to the interior of the store and winding its way to the right side of the shop to pass behind the existing window. The material continuity of the tiles not only serves to tie together the three distinct parts of the façade, but also becomes a subtly textured backdrop for the colourful contents.

Many intentional design decisions are incorporated to bring a touch of humanity to an otherwise sterile typology. Stepping into the store, the visitor does not immediately encounter the retail environment, but rather an art installation. Throughout the design process, we encouraged the client to break away from the convenience-store typology and dedicate a portion of the already small floor area to an undefined, multi-purpose exhibition space for showcasing artwork, installing feature brands, hosting pop-up events and accommodating large-scale visual merchandising. In the retail area, custom stainless-steel display and shelving fixtures envelop the perimeter completely. Stainless steel, a rather aseptic material, is brought to life by the layering of various finishes, including brushed and polished, perforated and bump-textured. The vibrant packaging of the products, the colours and shapes of the feature artwork and the signage lighting all reflect off each other, blurring boundaries and activating the space.

With this project, we attempt to refine and evolve the convenience-store typology, while fulfilling its inherent demand for efficiency and functionality. Every designed element, detail and material choice embodies the desire for more – perhaps, for a bit of gravitas to anchor ourselves in a fast-paced consumer environment.

shanghai

architectural renovation
interior
products
environmental graphics

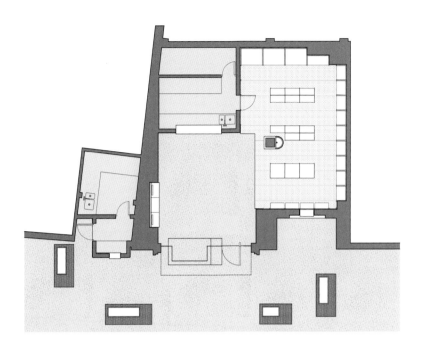

5 m (16½ ft)

2 3

4

the recontextualization of history
design commune and commune social

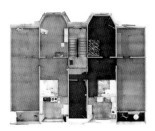

Andreas Gefeller, Untitled (Panel Building 4), *from* Supervisions *(2004)*

The hyperrealistic detail in Gefeller's photographs recalls the precision of an excavation. The way he meticulously combs surfaces and reveals minute traces of human intervention, a cigarette butt or a footprint, is similar to the way we approach an old building site. Also, the concept of stitching – Gefeller stitches together thousands of photos to create the final image – resonates with our idea of the way these smaller parts, details, build upon each other to form a whole new building.

shanghai

architectural renovation
interior
products
branding
environmental graphics

Built in 1909 in the International Settlement, the Gordon Road Police Station served as the headquarters for the Shanghai Municipal Police until 1943. Over the following decades, attempts were made by tenants to adapt the building for various uses, yet none of the interventions found an affinity with its colonial features. By the time it was added to a list of protected heritage buildings in 2005, it had been abandoned and fallen into disrepair. But the moment we came upon it, we sensed the vast potential of this building and immediately developed an obsession with transforming it into a design platform – a gathering space for designers and patrons alike to ponder, exchange and learn.

Working with a protected building, we liken the series of operations on its architecture to a surgical procedure. In this case, we first gently removed the decaying wood and plaster, carefully restoring portions of the still-vibrant red brickwork. Then, we grafted on skins (surfaces/partitions), joints (details/connectors) and organs (technical functions). And finally, with the attachment of a brand-new appendage – the glazed retail storefront on the ground floor – this metaphorical prosthetic enables a nearly abandoned building to perform again in a new capacity.

Contrasting with the exterior, which has been mostly left intact owing to historic preservation guidelines, the interior has been completely transformed. In many ways, these transformations are counterintuitive to the conventional role of the architect, which is to 'build'. This project should be discussed in terms of deletions rather than additions. Working within the mandate of preserving all existing structures, we identified opportunities for alterations. The straightforward plan and section of the existing building, with three stacked floors and a centralized spine for circulation, are disrupted as strategic cuts are made in the entry lobby and the main corridor. Seemingly minute, these manoeuvres convert a series of existing linear spaces into an interlocking puzzle of volumes. The new double-height spaces are lined with multiple glazed openings, each exposing a vignette of the rooms beyond, to activate visual connections and create spatial intrigues. Circulation patterns are forced to shift around these cut-outs, encouraging a visceral exploration rather than a journey guided by logic. These deceptively insignificant acts of interrogation effectively alter the spatial experience and become a catalyst for the evolution of this historic building, setting the stage for new possibilities of use and occupation.

There is an unspoken understanding that some things should remain unaltered. In dealing with the materiality, the challenge is actually to resist the urge to fix every imperfection, instead honouring the imprint of time on each surface. Though many of the original walls have been refinished with plaster, the original floor joists, the wooden roof structure and some doors are kept intact. Finally, this respect for the past plays out in an almost cinematic way in the attic. Picture this ethereal scene that we found during an early site visit: a small platform hovering among wood rafters, a ladder propped up in the centre, a solitary chair lying beside it, and light streaming through the collapsing roof. Captivated by this incidental staging of ordinary objects in a suspended moment, we recreate this sight in the attic, a space with no assigned function, as a quiet tribute to the many past and future lives relevant to this building.

former gordon road police station (1910)

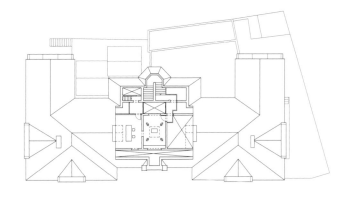

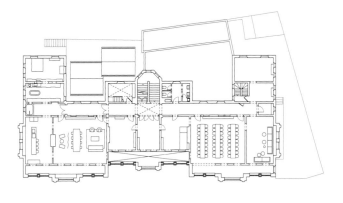

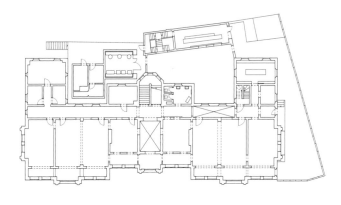

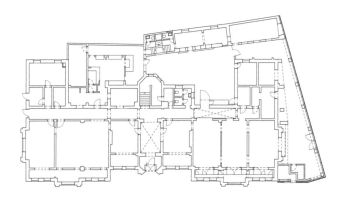

18 m (59 ft)

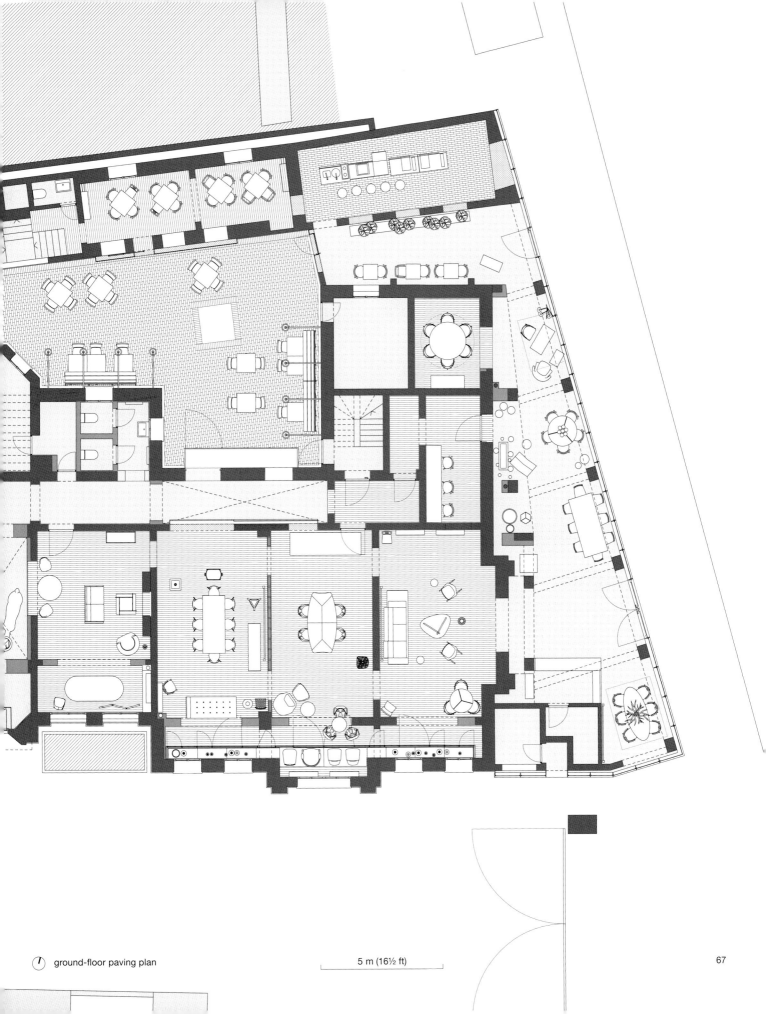

1 ground-floor paving plan

5 m (16½ ft)

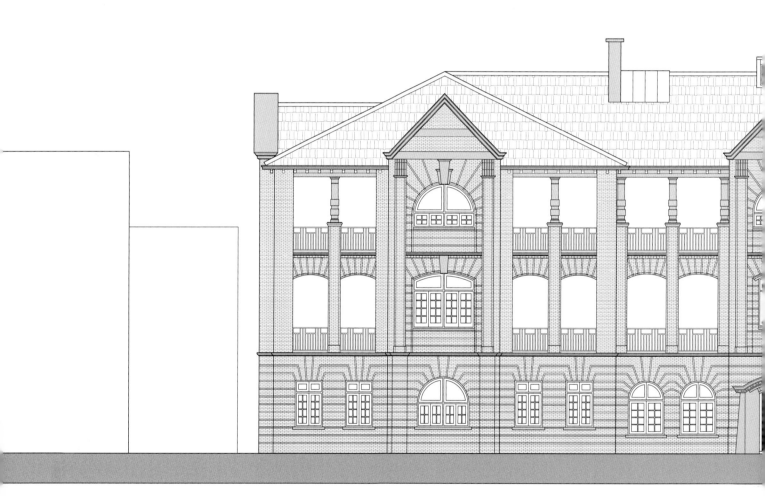

south elevation

5 m (16½ ft)

1

2

1 framed brick wall 2 vestibule atrium

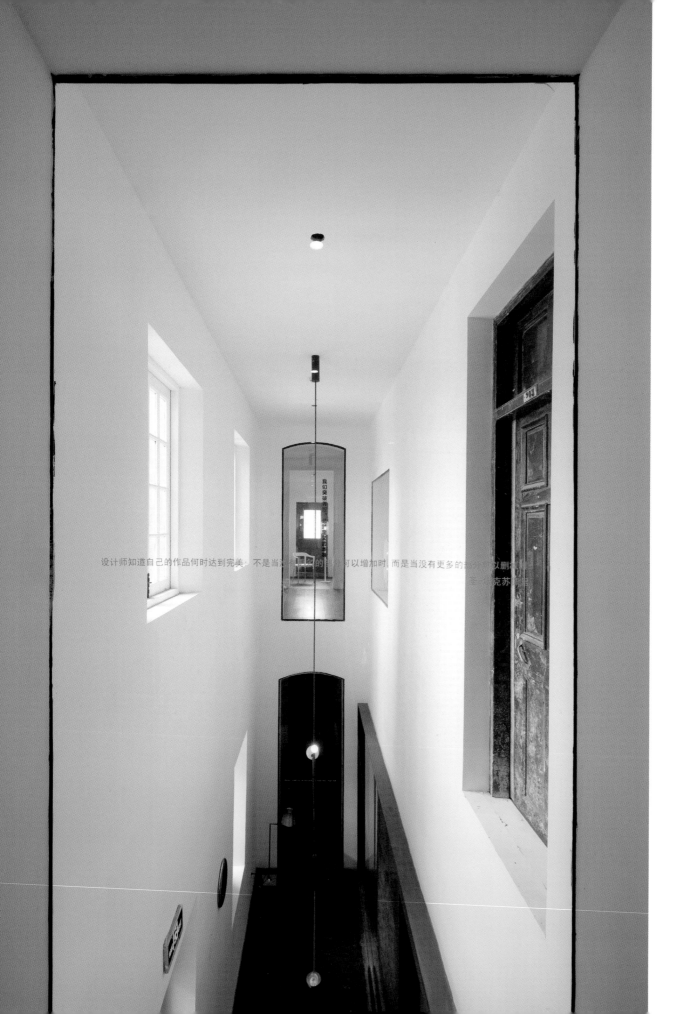

设计师知道自己的作品何时达到完美，不是当没有更多的部分可以增加时，而是当没有更多的部分可以删减时。
——安东尼·德·圣艾克苏佩里

3

4

5

4 event space 5 opening to manifesto gallery

6

7

DESSERT BAR
SPECIAL:

Creme Catalan
--- 55 RMB

Warm Chocolate
with blood Oranges
--- 55 RMB

Ice Cream + Sorbet
Per Scoop --- 15 RMB

Todays Pastry Chefs:
Kim, Tony + Damon.

the vertical lane house
waterhouse at south bund

Approaching the site, a Japanese army building from the 1930s, the history written all over its surfaces is easily visible. Thus, the real task of this project was to hold back in the restoration process and resist the natural urge to fix every flaw. We were very careful to delineate where new elements were to be inserted and where the old should remain untouched. While some of the spaces have been refinished and smoothed over, some portions of walls are left crude, exposing crumbling bricks and delicate lathwork behind the deteriorating plaster. Encased in a glass shield, these raw wall sections evoke the archival quality of a museum display, and suddenly the overlooked and mundane is elevated to the precious. Peeling back the layers of finishes is akin to performing an autopsy – uncovering the lives and narratives hidden within each imperfection, and excavating memories that will bring the most intimate moments of inhabitation to the public light.

Just as purposeful as respecting the demarcation between the old and the new is, conversely, erasing the boundary between the public and the private. We are interested in breaking down the visual, aural and physical limitations of personal space across various scales. This pursuit is manifested in the planning of the hotel's signature restaurant, which is an extension of the street all the way into the inner courtyard, so that the public realm penetrates deeply into the core of the private sphere. A cut in the ceiling of the restaurant even allows occupants of the guestrooms above to participate peripherally in the lively activity among the diners below. The seemingly misplaced windows throughout (such as the one above the main reception in the lobby), cleverly situated reflective surfaces and unexpected circulation paths offer the constant thrill of a stolen view and a wayward glimpse.

In its very conception, the Waterhouse seeks to question the typology of a hotel, how to interpret notions of 'home' and domesticity in a foreign environment, and how to give meaning to the experience of a traveller. To do so, we draw from the rich experience of a typical Shanghai *longtang* (lane or alley), where everyday living is full of discoveries and surprises, and where the concept of true privacy does not exist. By challenging the most basic rituals of daily life and transforming their familiarity into something wholly unpredictable, such as presenting bathing in a glass box, we amplify the constant play between notions of comfort and discomfort. These unexpected moments are meant to heighten the emotional journey of the guest. The graphic wall markings throughout the hotel space evoke and suggest the complexity of the traveller's psychological states – longing and exhilaration, uncertainty and desire, discomfort and relief – while the distinct rawness of the material palette establishes an intense sense of time, place and being.

shanghai

architectural renovation
interior
products
environmental graphics

1

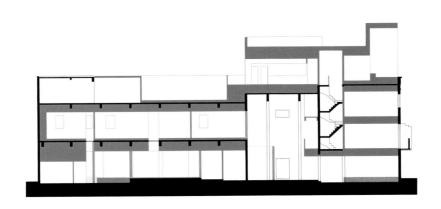

demolition plan | section

15 m (49 ft)

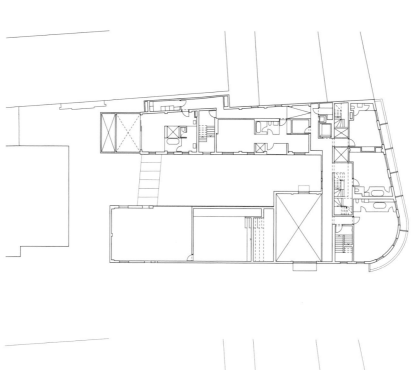

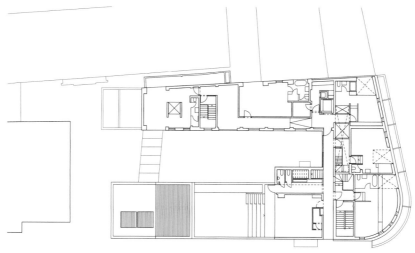

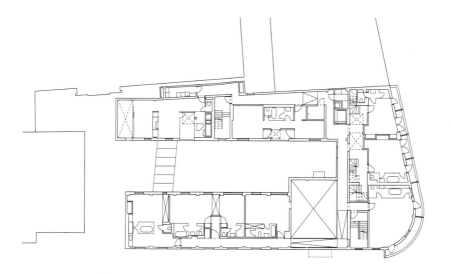

20 m (65½ ft)

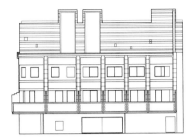

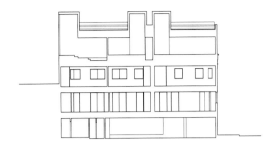

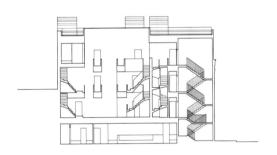

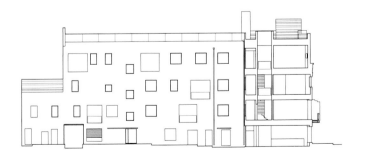

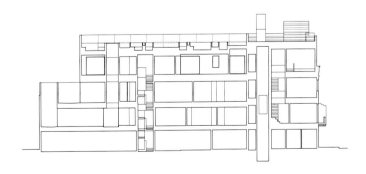

elevations I sections

20 m (65½ ft)

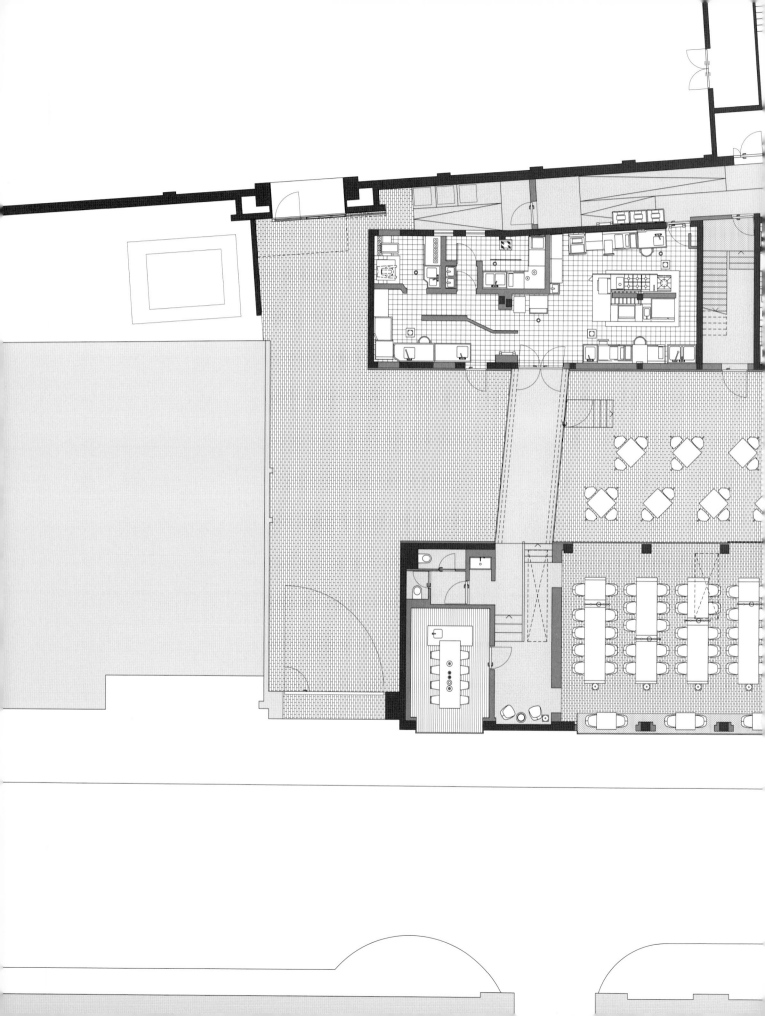

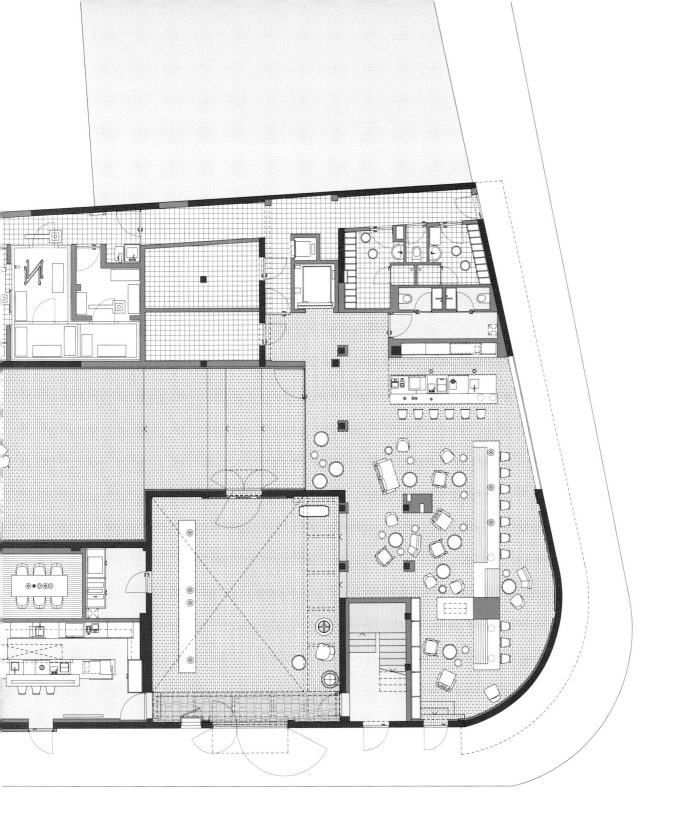

1 ground-floor paving plan

5 m (16½ ft)

1 Terrace floor assembly
20 mm (¾ in) wood floorboard
pressure-treated substructure
5 mm (¼ in) polythene membrane
50 mm (2 in) XPS rigid insulation
3 mm (⅛ in) vapour barrier
screed laid to falls
150 mm (6 in) new concrete slab
5 mm (¼ in) polythene membrane
45 mm (1¾ in) XPS rigid insulation

2 Wooden window
20 mm (¾ in) wood board
tensile steel cable cross bracing
6 mm (¼ in) fibre cement board
2 mm (⅛ in) stainless steel, chrome mirror finish
160 mm (6¼ in) cavity
6+15+6 mm (¼+⅝+¼ in) double glazing

3 Room floor and ceiling assembly
20 mm (¾ in) wood floorboard
20 mm (¾ in) plywood
40 mm (1⅝ in) battens
5 mm (¼ in) sound insulation
100 mm (4 in) existing concrete slab
50 mm (2 in) XPS insulation
3 mm (⅛ in) polythene membrane
250 mm (10 in) cavity
50 mm (2 in) V-channel
15 mm (⅝ in) gypsum board
45 mm (1¾ in) XPS insulation
3 mm (⅛ in) white render

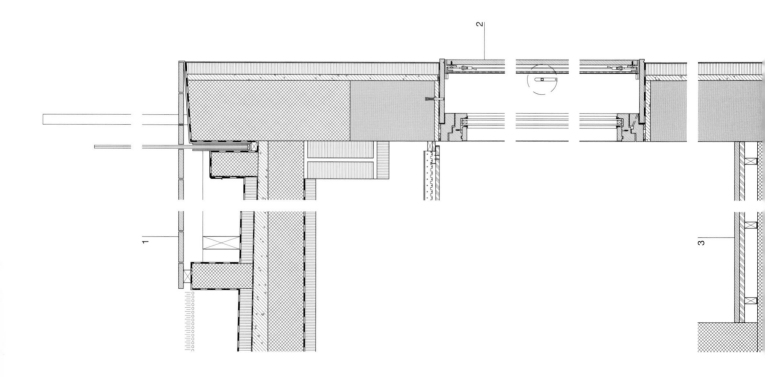

4 Wall assembly
white render
mesh glued to insulation
45 mm (1¾ in) XPS rigid board
25 mm (1 in) cement levelling
100 mm (4 in) existing concrete slab
50 mm (2 in) XPS insulation
3 mm (⅛ in) polythene membrane
250 mm (10 in) cavity
50 mm (2 in) V-channel
15 mm (⅝ in) gypsum board
45 mm (1¾ in) XPS insulation
3 mm (⅛ in) white render

5 Balcony floor assembly
18 mm (¾ in) wood floorboard
70 mm (2¾ in) battens with cavity
3 mm (⅛ in) polythene membrane
screed laid to falls, 5%
existing reinforced concrete slab

6 Wall assembly
5 mm (¼ in) white render
45 mm (1¾ in) XPS board
20 mm (¾ in) screed
240 mm (9½ in) existing brick wall
5 mm (¼ in) polythene membrane
45 mm (1¾ in) XPS board
20 mm (¾ in) wood baseboard

7 Floor assembly
20 mm (¾ in) wood floorboard
25 mm (1 in) battens
35 mm (1½ in) lightweight concrete topping
40 mm (1⅝ in) profiled steel sheet
150 mm (6 in) substructure with XPS rigid insulation
5 mm (¼ in) polythene membrane
existing concrete base

8 Courtyard ground assembly
86 mm (3½ in) recycled grey brick
20 mm (¾ in) mortar bed
55 mm (2¼ in) screed levelling
ACO brickslot
rammed earth

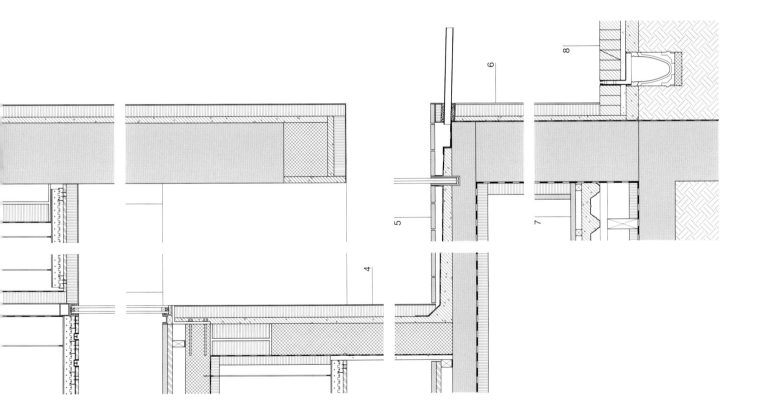

courtyard façade detail

0.1 m (4 in)   1 m (3¼ ft)

4

5

4 staircase connection 5 staircase detail

6

7

6 guestroom 7 hallway and balcony facing courtyard

8

9

10

11

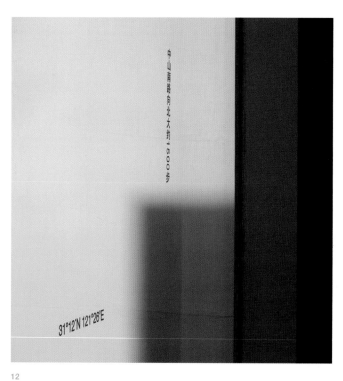

12

13

14

15

16

nomadic voyeurism

In contrast to most classical Western paintings, which are based on mimesis, Chinese *literati* paintings aim to capture the spirit of the object depicted, filtered through the lens of abstraction. Evoking the artist's inner landscape precedes imitation or approximation of nature. As an extension of the arts, classical Chinese gardens are a nexus of multiple disciplines: painting, literature, garden planning and horticulture, to name a few. Created as microcosms by the *literati* (scholar-gentlemen), the gardens are not meant to be revealed all at once and are designed around elements of concealment and surprise. The projects presented in this chapter capture how the technique of *jiejing*, or 'borrowed scenery', frequently found in Chinese gardens, offers novel ways of seeing that challenge our perceptions of fixed boundaries. These projects all exhibit part-to-whole relationships among a collective of fragments that are meant to be pieced together by the roving eye of the nomadic voyeur.

Sharing similarities but not to be conflated with voyeurism, *jiejing* departs from the conventional Western notion of voyeurism, which is associated with regimes of control and surveillance, focusing instead on the revelatory vantages gained by the nomadic inhabitant. To initiate a journey within a Chinese garden is to mediate a myriad contrasts, correspondences, views and circulations.[2] Traditionally, the borrowed view is a technique that blurs the boundaries between nature and artifice, plays with perspectival distance and curates a series of vignettes. Borrowed views defy accepted norms of viewing and exact visual transgressions (through screens, apertures and portals) that manipulate spatial depth and the perception of scale and distance. The projects shown in this chapter take lessons from the visual operatives of *jiejing* and voyeurism to create and tease out desire, anticipation and curiosity.

In Rethinking the Split House (p. 140), the inhabitant's gaze is constantly reoriented based on their journey around the central staircase, which mediates between domestic programmes of varying privacy. The nomadic voyeur is implied in Curio Stair of Encounters (p. 122), inspired by Hong Kong's urban terrain, where the coveted harbour view is purposefully denied upon first approach and slowly revealed as visitors circulate up. For the Archives (p. 128) and Muted Landscape (p. 134) hotel projects, the hypothetical traveller (as opposed to tourist) is reminiscent of the scholar who sojourns in the garden's varied landscapes and cultivates his mind through self-discovery. The Unfolding Village installation (p. 112) features screens, windows and shutters that create intriguing vignettes, capturing unexpected views. Lastly, in the Extroverted Privacy (p. 116), the nomad reappears in the domestic sphere, where the inversion of the typical urban loft diagram dislodges conventional notions of luxury and comfort. In a way, to be a nomad is not dissimilar to experiencing a literary narrative; by exploring limits of the nomadic gaze we indulge our fascination with voyeurism and all its tantalizing potentials to unlock new spatial awareness.

the unfolding village
installation design for stockholm furniture & light fair 2019

As guest of honour at the Stockholm Furniture & Light Fair 2019, we chose to design an installation that departed from the conventional aspirations of furniture fairs, which often focus only on displaying product designs. The Chinese notion of 'fiction' is historically assigned to the term *xiaoshuo*, literally translated as 'small talk' originating from the stories and gossip heard in alleys and streets.[3] Building on our research into the roots underpinning Chinese culture, we used this installation to highlight the issue of disappearing villages by employing a spatial organization that transforms the traditional 'street' into a narrative device.

The pressing issue we wanted to highlight is China's alarming trend of disappearing villages, which signifies the erosion of the traditional notions of community, family and cultural roots. With 80 per cent of its intangible cultural heritage coming from rural origins, once the villages disappear, the country risks losing its memories and witnesses of its cultural heritage. As many of our product designs are informed by notions of nostalgia, dwelling, home, family and the individual's relationship within a collective, we wanted to create an installation built upon the essence of the traditional Chinese village. Inspired by the alleyway and street life of clan-based villages, the exhibition layout takes the form of a sinuous and continuous alleyway, which unfolds to create lanes and layers of spaces slowly revealing themselves to visitors. The profile and form take on the reading of an abstracted pitched roof, which symbolizes home, and when repeated in connected rows forms a 'village'.

The locally sourced pine wood is painted black, evoking the village as a silhouette of withered memory. Placed in a curated dialogue with each other, objects such as furniture, lighting and accessories that would typically be appreciated solely for their aesthetic value can now take on greater meanings. As the visitor moves through the space, screens and openings frame views from the communal streetscape. Vantage points compress and release, guiding visitors through and piquing their curiosity to explore. Playing on the idea that fair visitors would converge to form a temporary 'village community', we deploy the spatial device of the alley as a quirky tableau for object display, inviting the subversive behaviours of gossip, voyeurism and eavesdropping. Ultimately, the exhibition is much more than a mere platform to present beautiful objects: it is a true opportunity to generate discussions in the international design community regarding social and cultural issues, which are at once local and universal in this age of hectic mass development.

stockholm

installation
graphic collaterals
environmental graphics

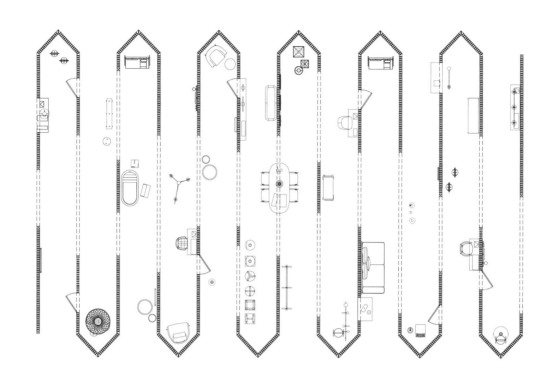

plan

|— 5 m (16½ ft) —|

落葉寒蟬小巷深
枯藤斜日半墻陰

——秋晚東海寓舍 袁凱

the extroverted privacy
wu residence

This 250 m² (2,690 sq ft) private residence project in a highrise tower in the heart of Singapore is the result of the client's seemingly simple mandate: 'Give me three bedrooms and a project that will challenge the conventional notion of what a flat should be.' Rising to this challenge, we initiated the project by questioning the fundamentals of the 'house' typology itself, asking ourselves: How can we free up the plan and make it feel light and loft-like? What is the relationship between the communal and the private? When and how should privacy be maintained, if at all? What are the essential and nonessential programme components that make a 'home'? What is domesticity?

The resulting parti (the primary organizing idea behind a design) breaks through all conventions of the standard apartment layout by placing the rooms away from the building edge, reserving a continuous corridor along the entire perimeter. Rather than entering the centre and then radiating outward towards individual rooms, which is a configuration often taken for granted as the ideal condition in highrise residences, here the private zone forms the core of the space, while the public circulation zone envelops and ties everything together. The strategic insertion of three free-floating volumes, clad in wood, stone and copper, adds to the depth of the spatial layers, enclosing within them the most private and intimate rooms of all – the study and the two bathrooms. The remaining space is kept transparent, pushing the boundary of how open and extroverted a room can be while still maintaining privacy. The project rejects the parcelization of spaces typically found in apartment layouts, creating an openness and expansiveness that is more conducive to a contemporary lifestyle.

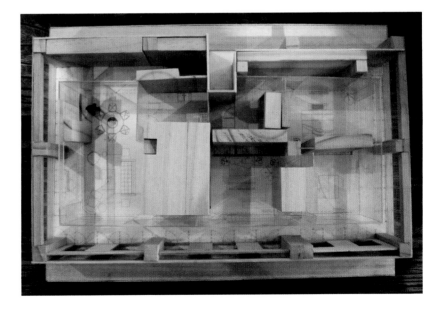

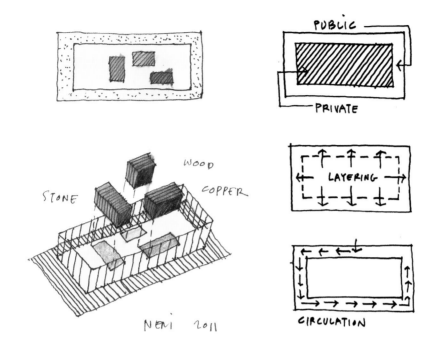

STONE   WOOD

COPPER

NEM   2011

PUBLIC

PRIVATE

LAYERING

CIRCULATION

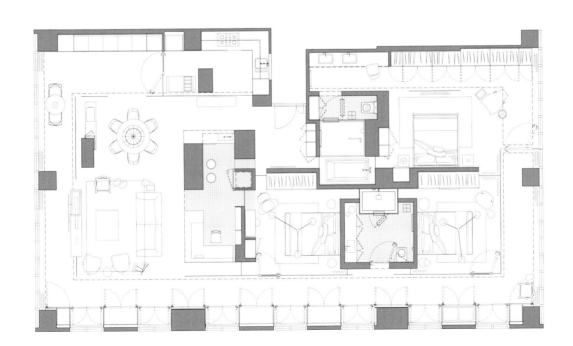

1

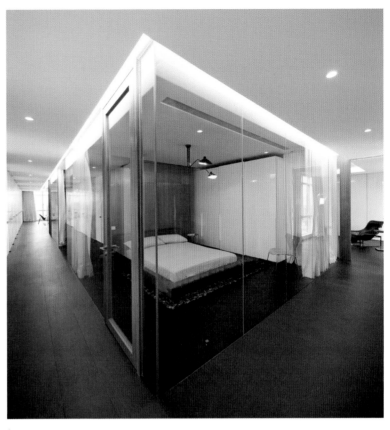

2

3

curio stair of encounters
bloomberg hong kong office

In his 1978 essay 'Figures, Doors and Passages', Robin Evans analyses how the ordinary elements of a plan interact and shape occupancy. A simple corner or window opening is, in fact, inscribed with a complex matrix of spatial relationships that determine how a space is used. Our design for Bloomberg Hong Kong's internal office stairs was in part inspired by the mundane elements of space-making: windows, passages, staircases and thresholds. The challenge was to redesign a staircase that worked within the structural limitations of the knock-out panels in the floor slab, while creating a spacious journey.

The staircase integrates platforms and built-in seating, composed as a landscape that echoes Hong Kong's natural and urban terrains. Expressed as a wooden box insertion, the massing consciously denies views to the Victoria Harbour, instead focusing on the activities within. Enclosed in a light ash wood massing, with exposed aggregate concrete treads and metal rail accents, the staircase winds and turns to offer unexpected views. Each of the three levels is designed with different functions to accommodate a diverse set of vertical programmes. The journey begins on the twenty-fifth-floor reception level, which is designed to be the most extroverted in nature, with a large event space stage, built-in benches on the perimeter, and dedicated areas for small break-out group seating. On closer interaction with the millwork, hidden bespoke details are revealed to the user – fold-out panels for charging ports, mirrors and functional ledges, supporting the daily rituals of office life.

Continuing up, the mass splits into two boxes, accentuating the landing as a threshold that visually opens up to the harbour view along the curtain wall. On the final level, the staircase opens up again to be more extroverted, bringing in views of the office surroundings. The massing is reduced further in scale, punctuated with larger openings and clear glass to provide expansive views out to the harbour. A cantilevered viewing podium provides dramatic views down multiple levels, as the journey culminates in a lounge facing the harbour once again. Through careful composition and juxtaposition, the ordinary vignettes in an office typology we take for granted on a daily basis are choreographed into a rich journey that allows for moments of chance encounter, pause and informal conversation.

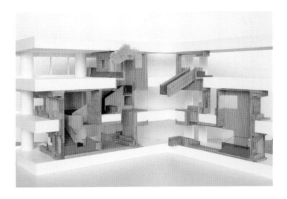

hong kong

interior
products
environmental graphics

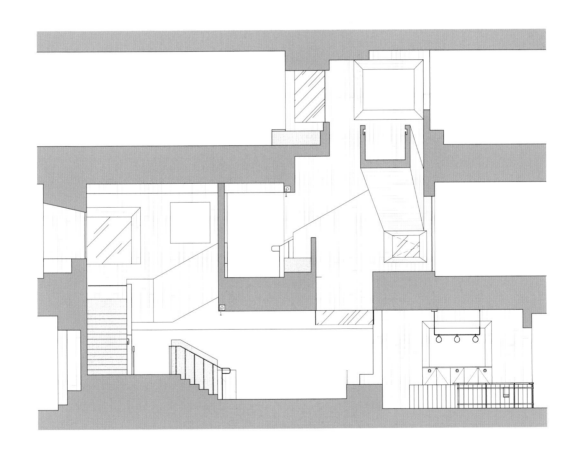

section

5 m (16½ ft)

1

2

the archives
le méridien zhengzhou

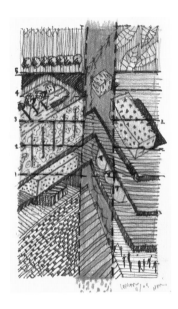

The Zhongyuan (Central Plain) area, centred on Henan Province and radiating throughout the middle and lower reaches of the Yellow River, was one of the main cradles of Chinese civilization. Our design for the Le Méridien Hotel in Zhengzhou, the nucleus of Henan Province, is a song of praise to this locality that marks the nation's cultural birth. Using the formal language of the box as an overarching motif, we conceived of the building as an archive of new and old cultural artefacts categorized in different boxes, acting as a point of discovery for residents of and travellers to this city alike. Each box contains a specific functional programme linked to a particular theme to showcase the region's history through its arts of literature, nature, food, theatre and pattern. Together, these various boxes form a rich layering of cultural treasures, a collective container of narratives that weave together plots and polar contrasts.

Externally, the cantilevered, stacked bronze boxes are carefully composed on the façade, with subtle slab-depth variations to break down the bulky proportion of the inherited building structure, while green glazing of various tints exaggerates depth variations. The volumes of the boxes are brought into the interior, as the same bronze panels extend to articulate enclosures demarcating entrances and ceiling planes. Visitors are greeted off the street though a forest of bronze poles marking the entry threshold. After passing through the arrival lobby they reach a four-storey atrium clad in striated grey sandstone. Inspired by the nearby Longmen Caves – one of the finest examples of Chinese Buddhist art, carved in limestone cliffs – we applied a language of excavation and carving to visually connect public functions across multiple levels. The top of the atrium is capped with a delicate articulation of dark timber boxes that fold down on to the uppermost level walls. This coffered ceiling allows skylights to pierce the space with shafts of natural light, highlighting the sedimentary pattern on the stone-clad walls.

To counter the banal repetition of typical hotel corridors, the guestroom tower features a series of stacked three-storey atriums, which are reserved for art installations. Each atrium features a unique installation taking on different themes varying from 'Myth' to 'Nature' to 'Culture', taking advantage of the spatial verticality to give each guestroom floor a unique visual fragment of the story. Another narrative device is the contrast of light and dark, a noteworthy theme we explore in the guestrooms. The living room and sleeping area are defined by a palette of grey plaster and dark-stained timber wainscot, while the minimalist bathrooms are clad in white glazed tiles and enclosed by a glass panel etched with a Henan *yueji* flower, a motif that is repeated on the building façade in a perforated back-lit pattern.

Le Méridien is our first attempt at a large-scale project with a heavily interdisciplinary approach. If the essence of story-telling can be understood as an attentive art of assemblage, of piecing together fragments that are of various origins, times, mediums and senses, then Le Méridien is our effort to tell a complex story on the most comprehensive scale – an experiment to materialize heritage, manifested in every aspect of the hotel.

zhengzhou

architecture
interior
products
environmental graphics

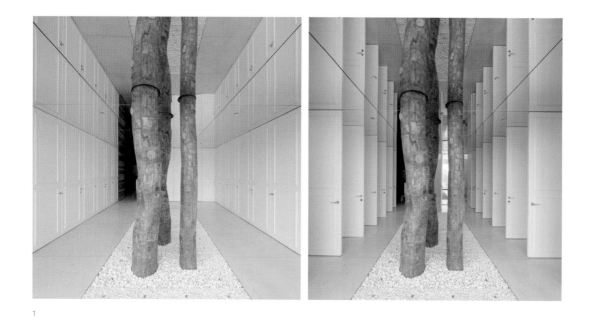

1

the muted landscape
the sukhothai shanghai

1

The Sukhothai hotel in Shanghai is an introverted fortress in the middle of the city's urban clamour, offering momentary insulation to travellers seeking a space of refuge away from the dramas of daily life. This project is an externalization of an abstracted inner landscape, a hushed zone in both its physical environment and the mentality it evokes. Throughout the public spaces of the hotel, the omnipresent sense of enclosures created with wooden screens and translucent layers of curtains cocoons the guests during their sojourn, creating a psychological distance away from the city. The introspective atmosphere is echoed by intricate details that take a quiet yet alert mind to appreciate, as well as the various nature motifs that bring the guests closer to the origin of the hotel's name *Sukhothai*, an early kingdom that flourished in the thirteenth to fifteenth centuries in north-central Thailand, with its abundant and varied features of nature.

Guests are greeted with a long reception desk set in front of a blank stone wall. Adjacent lies the hotel lobby, where grey terrazzo slabs are stacked, which begin to shift as they rise, forming a grand staircase that gives the illusion that guests are stepping on floating stairs. Lightweight bronze handrails are attached delicately, embellishing the staircase and reinforcing its sense of dynamism. Above, a wooden lantern-like structure hovers and envelops the space. The woven latticework of the lantern acts as a backdrop, suspending a series of custom bronze and glass pendant fixtures, making the guests feel as if they are walking into a forest of glowing lights.

In the public areas, the planning follows a series of metaphorical landscapes that change depending on the programme. The abstracted landscapes vary from adhering to classical notions of order and hierarchy, expressed with gridded columns and hanging lights, to more organic forms found in nature, which are translated into rich material applications with custom terrazzo and glazed tiles. Different zones are carved out with a sense of permeability. Rooms are not necessarily walled off, and the main dining space is open to the lobby and entry. And as guests wander around, they can find built-in seating that defines different pockets of space as one sees in a park or garden. The same motif of landscape continues into the guestrooms. An extended garden path leads guests to their own retreats on the upper floors. Within each guestroom, the private domain is conceived as an individual 'house', defined by thick stone walls and a gridded ceiling stricture, with the entire guestroom becoming an autonomous landscape that accommodates living functions within. Further beyond the 'house', the interior space opens up to create an intimate courtyard that captures natural light, framing an introspective view.

The Sukhothai Shanghai evokes the pleasure and peace one has when immersed in nature, but it is not another clichéd call to return to nature. It is a conscious design contingent upon an existing tower structure, its set limitations and the urban conditions that we attempt to mediate. Any urban traveller or city dweller would understand the preciousness of an urban fortress that protects that piece of quiet introspection that is often lacking in bustling cities.

shanghai

interior
products
environmental graphics

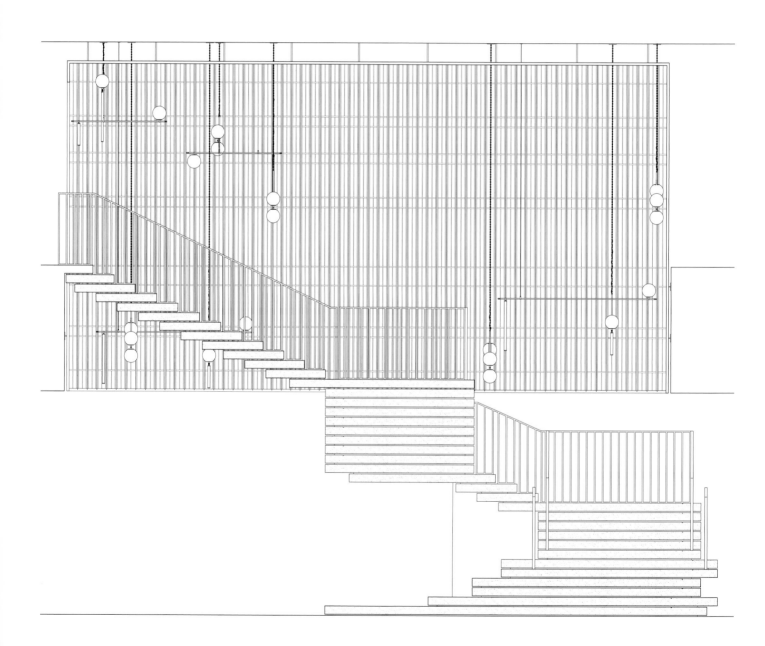

section

3 m (10 ft)

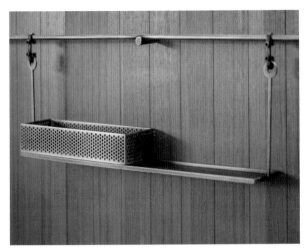

2

3

4

5

6

7

8

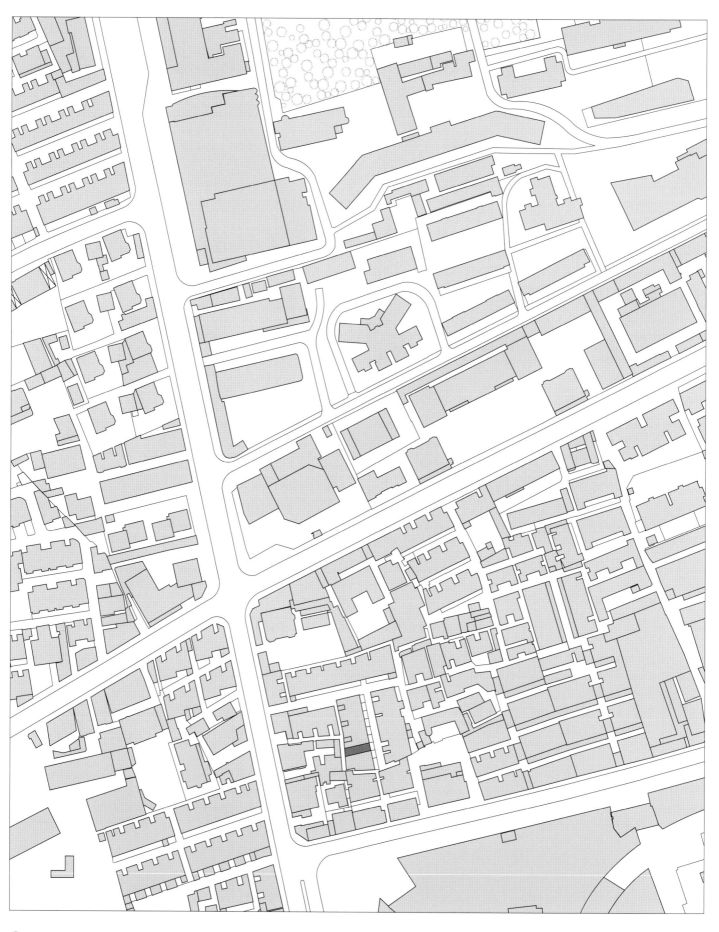

rethinking the split house
private residence in tianzifang

Alfred Hitchcock, Rear Window *(1954)*

The film explores the fascination with looking and the attraction of that which is being looked at. The constructed (fictional) environment of the film shares an uncanny similarity with the living conditions we find in Shanghai. The traditional alleys, called longtangs *– filled with secrets, desires and memories – are authentic models of Chinese urbanity and domesticity.*

The *longtang* lane house of Shanghai once comprised the dominant urban fabric that made Shanghai the intoxicating metropolis that it was in the 1930s. Being slowly demolished and eclipsed by high-density developments all over the city, the *longtang* is now a diminishing typology. One such dilapidated lane house that we were commissioned to reconstruct, located in the historic and artistic area of Tianzifang, was left with almost nothing except the existing shell. Our strategy was to rethink the typology of the lane house. The result is to keep the split-level formation and add spatial layering through new insertions and openings, at once retaining the architectural integrity of the typology while contemporizing it for today's lifestyle.

Historically, a lane house is separated into two distinct zones: a longer and often rectangular space, and a smaller room that is half a level above, creating a split section connected by a winding stairway in between. The lane houses, which used to be occupied by single families, have evolved over the course of the city's economic development, and now are typically occupied by three or more families. These households within a single lane house share the public staircase and landings, so the neighbours living on different levels or in separate rooms have a chance to interact as they move in and out of their personal spaces.

To keep this spirit alive, a new continuous metal stair was inserted to replace the old, decaying wooden stair that was no longer code-compliant. It serves as both the vertical access to all three levels and a horizontal link between the front room and the room half a level above, in line with the original spatial configuration. However, deviating from convention, all toilet facilities are now inserted into the split-level stair spaces to maintain the purity of the main rooms. These bathrooms, conceivably the most intimate spaces of an apartment, are immediately adjacent to the most public stairway, separated only by a translucent glass divider. The focal stair, which celebrates the blurring of the private and the public, is the conceptual departure point of the project, binding together the scattered spaces while bringing vibrancy and life to what is normally the darkest portion of the lane house.

Architecturally, the ornamentations built up over the façade in the last sixty years are stripped off, and large, glazed openings are created on the frontal section to bring light into the deepest part of the plan on each floor. Muted black paint is selected to de-emphasize the exterior form, drawing attention to the glowing apertures that link to the inside. Gazing into these picture windows, like the ones in Hitchcock's *Rear Window*, one is compelled to question notions of privacy, domesticity and community that constitute the unique environment of Shanghai's *longtang*. In contrast to the traditional lane house, where the interior organizations are suppressed on the exterior, these windows are a bold departure that reveal the architectural contents within. The visual transparency extends the voyeuristic gaze into the domestic interior, inviting stray glances from neighbouring homes into this intimate labyrinth. By capturing the spirit of the historical past and making modern abstract insertions to fit contemporary living, we hope to infuse new vibrancy to the lane house typology, whose original fabric seems to be dissolving too fast and too soon.

shanghai

architectural renovation
interior

entry exterior

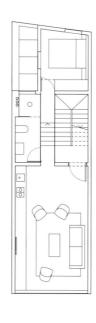

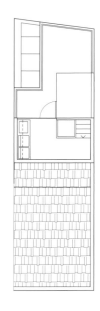

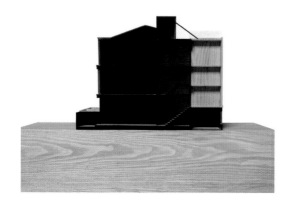
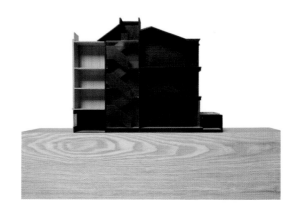

8 m (26¼ ft)

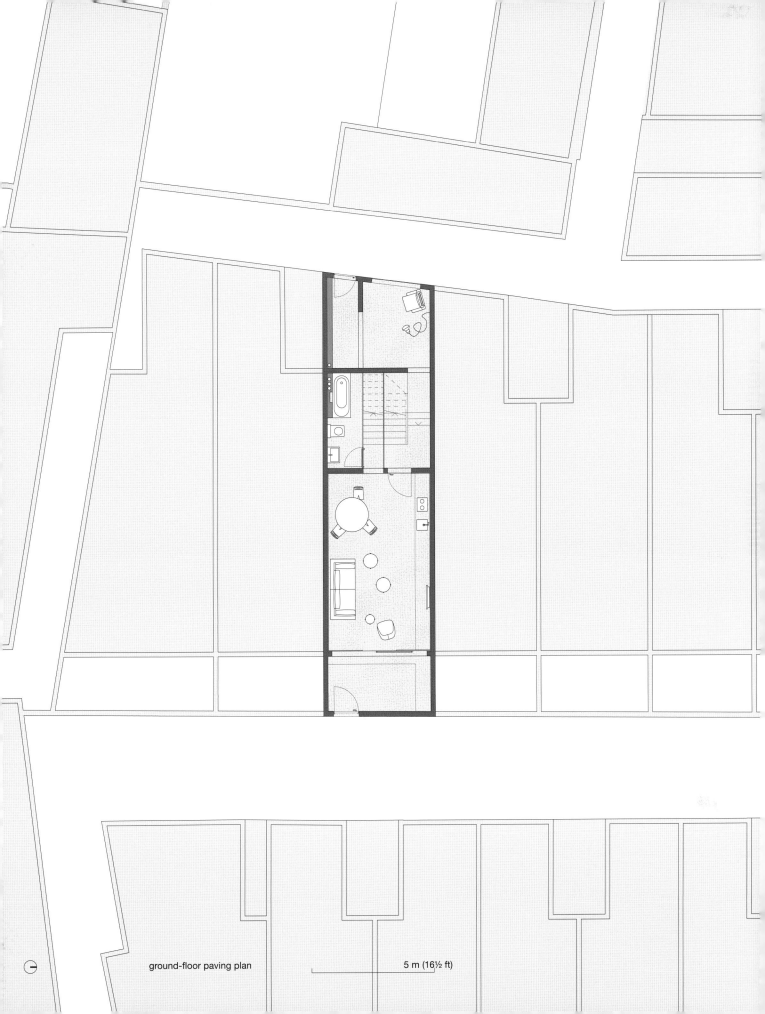

ground-floor paving plan

5 m (16½ ft)

1   2

3

4

5

dwelling

The notions of 'home' and being 'at home' are psychological constructs shaped by subjective perceptions of shelter, privacy, intimacy and sense of security. Dwellings bear the markings of our daily rituals of inhabitation, and over time they serve as vessels for the accumulated artefacts of our everyday lives. Beyond serving as containers and backdrops for life, dwellings are expressions of our values, drawing from our most intimate planes of existence and personal attachments. Although often linked to domesticity, dwelling is a nomadic concept unconstrained by programme and locale. According to the philosopher Martin Heidegger, we build only after we are capable of dwelling; dwellings are the physical manifestations of our impulse to find rootedness in the world. The layered meanings assigned to the word 'dwelling', originating from *dwellan* in Old English, have evolved over time, being associated with 'seduction, hindering, to lead astray and lingering', before the more recent meaning of 'to make a home' and to represent a place where one resides. As described by the Gaston Bachelard, the tension between house and universe results in a rivalry – the house resists the hostilities of the universe, declaring its insistence on inhabiting the world 'in spite of the world'.[4] Based on this tension, if a boundary is taken as the point where 'presencing' begins and not a point of termination,[5] then we believe that the power of dwelling is rooted in the notion of contrast – that its opposition to a general condition of a non-dwelling experience heightens its ability to reveal the dialectics of life.

Refuge, respite and introversion characterize many of the spaces shown in the following category; however, the idea of inner retreat is not to be taken as a rejection of external life. To appreciate dwelling one needs rupture, a moment of removal from the generic and mundane. In commercial projects such as Constellation of Enclosures (boutique shop; p. 154) and the Covered Hearth (high-end restaurant; p. 170), we introduce elements of domesticity such that moments of domestic life share a continuity with our urban sojourns. Our hotel projects illustrate the distinction between a tourist and a traveller as described by Paul Bowles in his novel *The Sheltering Sky* (1949): we embrace an imagined traveller 'belonging no more to one place than to the next … [who would find] it difficult to tell, among the many places he had lived, precisely where it was he had felt most at home.'[6] Bachelard's notion of the home as a repository of memories and daydreams, requisite for cultivating humanity's imagination, is explored in the Attic (creative consultancy office; p. 160), where a hideaway loft space is designed to invite staff to indulge in a brief moment of pause, and rediscover the excitement and childhood joy of hide and seek. Finally, dwelling's function to connect us back to nature and each other is captured in the House of Remembrance (p. 184), where a central garden memorializes a loved one lost, a spatial focal point that gathers collective experience while also providing individual refuge.

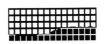

constellation of enclosures
jisifang boutique

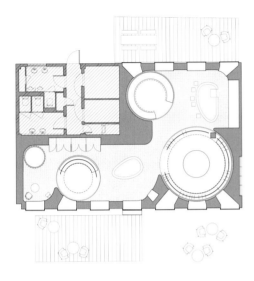

plan

The Jisifang Boutique is located in Shanghai's Columbia Circle, a revitalized compound consisting of preserved colonial monuments and former industrial buildings dating back to the 1920s. Sitting at the corner of the site, this boutique for a fabric manufacturer turned fashion brand occupies the ground floor of a post-industrial building – an urban artefact featuring an existing utilitarian concrete façade. The driving concept for the project centres on the studied relationship between architecture and fashion, and the unusual application of suspended textiles to define spatial enclosure.

The storefront, which is oriented towards a public plaza, is composed of a series of regularly spaced deep vertical windows. The exterior walls are treated as a thick, continuous encasing shell, which is then punched at regular intervals, creating apertures that seduce the visitor to explore the interior. The interior, in contrast, abandons any rectilinear geometry and is instead composed of a series of circular, spatial focal points. The departure for the interior concept is based on the nineteenth-century German architectural theorist Gottfried Semper's notion of the primitive textile wall as one of the four irreducible elements of architecture, which is a rejection of the conventional origin story of the primitive hut as the archetype underpinning architectural thinking.[7] Returning to the hung textile as a means of enclosure, we explore and highlight the brand's unique heritage in fabric-making.

Once inside the store, visitors find themselves immersed in a constellation of suspended, cylindrical fabric 'lanterns' that form pockets of enclosure. Despite being made of virtually weightless fabric, the hung partitions vary in scale and character to give each retail zone a unique spatial identity. Each 'lantern' demarcates a category within the brand's oeuvre and provides a contemplative space that harmonizes and celebrates its diverse contents. These luminescent enclosures are distributed in the plan to contain different functions: a private changing room, an area displaying home goods, and a large 7 m (23 ft)-diameter showroom with a central display table. Hung from circular wooden plates, the draping walls simultaneously provide a muted backdrop to foreground the hanging garments within and obscure visual clutter from the larger context. As the visitor walks around the fabric screens, the layers of sheer drapery at the same time delineate and blur thresholds.

The space is carefully assembled from a natural palette of organic cotton, light oak, matte tile, raw steel, reclaimed brick and unfinished concrete. The ground and the encasing walls carry a sober character in opposition to the airiness of the lanterns. The ground plane is treated like a heavy earthwork finished in concrete and concentric patterns of reclaimed bricks. At times rising to become tables, the brick floor creates an interior landscape playing on the tension between the heavy and the ephemeral, the stereotomic and the tectonic. Lined with fluted ivory-coloured terracotta bricks, the perimeter walls are treated as a thickened poché (on a plan, the solid spaces between walls) that binds the curvilinear forms in the interior to the rationally spaced apertures on the façade. Through a series of visual and sensory contrasts, we create an intimate ambience that requires both feeling and contemplation, through a profound understanding of materiality.

shanghai

interior
products

1

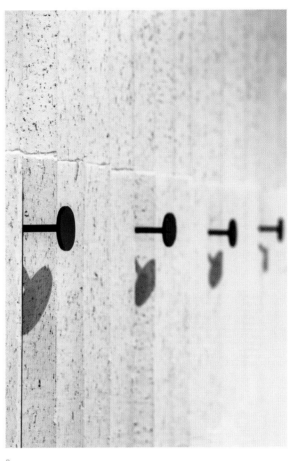

2

3

4

the attic
flamingo shanghai office

In Gaston Bachelard's seminal work *The Poetics of Space* (1958), he proposes a metaphor of the house as a dwelling for the psyche. While the subterranean cellar represents our deep subconscious, the elevated attic is a space of quiet and rational thought. In our imaginations and memories, the attic is an oft-forgotten space, a space of contradictions and possibilities: both dark and light, intimate and vast, daunting and comforting. Our renovation of an industrial roof space in Shanghai into an office for a leading global insight and strategic consultancy, Flamingo, was inspired by these paradoxical and enigmatic notions of the attic.

Essentially a flat roof converted into an inhabitable space with the addition of a steel A-frame structure, the site itself was a main driver for the design intent. We aimed to exaggerate and enhance the experience of the existing condition; that is, of occupying the space within the eaves of a roof, like an attic. The insertion of house-like volumes into a landscape of concrete platforms breaks down the homogeneous space, so that the roof is not just a singular element, but can be experienced on multiple levels, from various vantage points and on various scales.

Traversing the open work area, one first experiences an extensive view of the original structure, while black metal mesh panels frame bright clerestory windows above. The exhibition area features a floating roof form above to encapsulate the entire space while leaving it open and flexible. The board room, on the other hand, is completely enclosed, but also captures the double-pitched roof and features lighting fixtures that mimic natural skylights. As a culmination of the attic experience, a narrow set of stairs brings one to a small mezzanine level, where a hidden room is nestled within the larger ones, its windows offering stolen glimpses into other rooms – a moment to reflect in hindsight upon the spaces once occupied.

The project brief included several pairs of rooms divided by one-way mirrors for research-based observation. Expanding upon notions of voyeurism, the interspersed application of varying types of glass – clear glass, frosted glass and one-way mirrors – forces the occupants into a state of slight discomfort, as the roles of the observer and the observed may be reversed at any given turn. Through carefully crafted openings and layered materials, each enclosure becomes a viewing mechanism in Beatriz Colomina's sense – 'a viewing mechanism that produces the subject... precedes and frames the occupant',[8] which is a property of architecture that serves as a filter through which we examine others as we examine ourselves.

shanghai

interior
products
environmental graphics

1

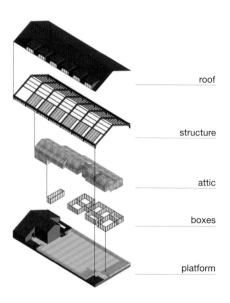

roof

structure

attic

boxes

platform

2

3

4

the urban oasis
alila bangsar

1

Embodied as a luxuriant mingling of a grid structure and integrated lush planting within, Alila Bangsar challenges the artificial separation of architecture and nature, and instead aims to merge a rational sensibility with the organic pulse of the locality. Our hotel project is situated at the junction between two former colonial neighbourhoods of Kuala Lumpur – Brickfields, known as Little India, and the up-and-coming area of Bangsar; while connecting the current context to the location's past memories, it also connects the interior with the exterior, the curated to the unaffected.

A rigorous structural grid defines the hotel's external and internal logic; it organizes the façade while acting as a framework within which the internal functions of the hotel are contained. On the ground floor, guests are welcomed into the lower lobby through regular intervals of the grid. Upon entering, they are immediately immersed in a lush landscape of tree plantings throughout the interior. Once arriving at the upper lobby on the forty-first level, guests are met by a double-height space – an open-air 'light-well' that maximizes natural daylight intake while providing an extended view into the urban landscape of Kuala Lumpur. The presence of nature is further highlighted by the introduction of a water element, in the form of a swimming pool, into the centre of this uncovered atrium. Extending from the lobby space, a theatrical grand staircase, which is in itself also a stage that invites performances, descends to the pool. The total effect of this dramatic space is a sensorial experience where mind and body are transported through the unexpected mingling of natural and manmade elements, articulated as a rational, unrelenting structural grid.

The structural grid opens up to form a courtyard around which all activities within the hotel are centred, catalysing a reconfiguration of the opposition between what is conventionally deemed interior and artificial and what is usually regarded as exterior and organic. Spanning three storeys, the public areas surrounding the central courtyard are defined by a regular grid of columns and beams that frame views of the stunning panorama, while cradling the inserted courtyard in the density of the surrounding metropolis. Custom furniture and crafted bronze details complement the simple material palette of grey stone, white plaster and balau wood, providing the oasis with soft tones and handcrafted textures.

Two elements underpin the design of the guestrooms: 'the hut' and 'the indoor courtyard', which extend the blurring of the interior and the exterior. Following the analogy of a small village formed by the aggregation of guestrooms, the hut serves as the indoor space where the functions of daily living are enclosed. The bathroom is inserted as a floating box within the hut structure and allows for free-flowing circulation around its periphery. On the other hand, the indoor courtyard at the end of the room close to the window becomes a private sanctuary for guests to enjoy the exquisite views of Bangsar and beyond.

kuala lumpur

architectural renovation
interior
products
environmental graphics

1 aerial view

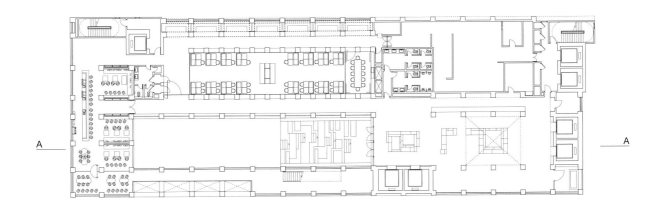

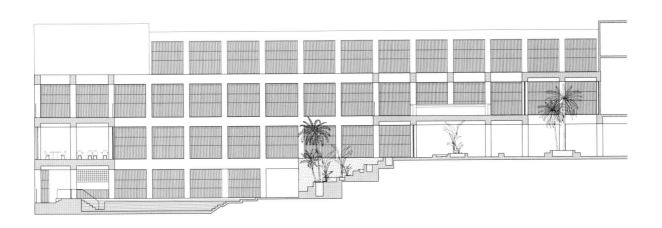

floor plan I section

20 m (65½ ft)

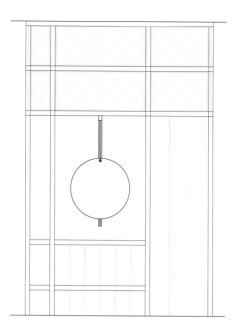

mirror 1:50

bar chair 1:20

lounge chair 1:20

2

custom furniture

the covered hearth
chi-q at three on the bund

Primitive notions of shelter, enclosure and the symbolism of the hearth are explored in our design for a restaurant located in Shanghai's historic Three on the Bund. Chi-Q was designed for renowned chef Jean-Georges Vongerichten and represents his unique interpretation of traditional Korean cuisine. The cuisine offered is an upscale version of the classic Korean barbecue, a programmatic typology where the act of cooking and eating converges around multiple sources of fire within the dining space. Inspired by the presence of fire, an element that conjures primordial associations with the warmth and shelter centred on the hearth, we aimed to create a dining experience that celebrates the formation of communal bonds through food.

The design is composed of three key elements and stems from a negotiation between contrasting yet complementary impulses, emphasizing a balance between raw materiality and refined craftsmanship. The 'hearth and mound' is represented in an interior landscape of partially sunken seating; the 'enclosure' is found in the form of screens; and finally a hovering 'shed roof' unifies all the elements together under one, figurative home. Clad in charcoal wood slats and custom concrete floors, the entrance is reminiscent of the discrete entrance found in a traditional Korean house. Upon crossing the threshold of a wooden gate, guests are greeted with a sliding wooden door, which reveals a long bar offering views on to an interior garden-scape. Half-sunken banquettes lead diners to a communal table located under the atrium, now articulated as a unifying roof structure that establishes the vertical void as the heart of the project. Floating within this void is a series of custom pendant lights, delicately suspended as glass orbs to animate the darkened interior. Extensive materials research was conducted for custom samplings of cast concrete with aggregate, large hand-carved patterned oak floors, oxidized raw-steel panels, custom pendant lighting, and charcoal *shousugiban* wood panels. Materiality and lighting create a meditative atmosphere that balances an earthiness with a sophisticated restraint that appeals to all the senses – visual, aural and haptic.

shanghai

interior
products
branding
environmental graphics

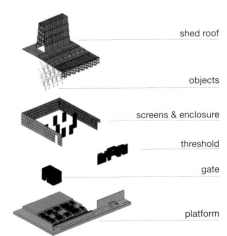

shed roof

objects

screens & enclosure

threshold

gate

platform

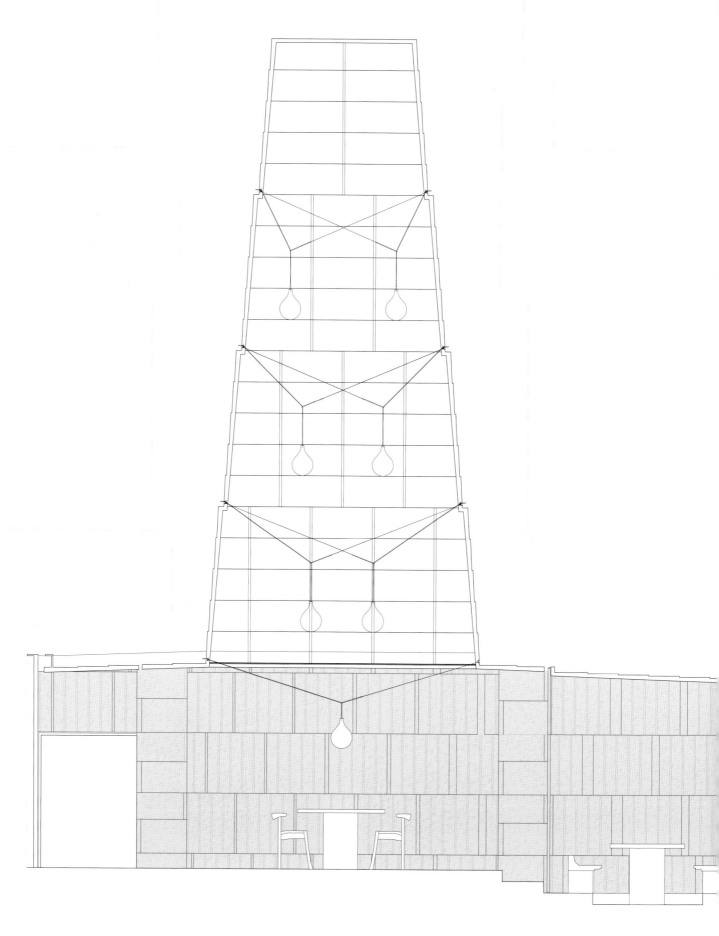

section   ┠─── 2 m (2½ ft) ───┨   172

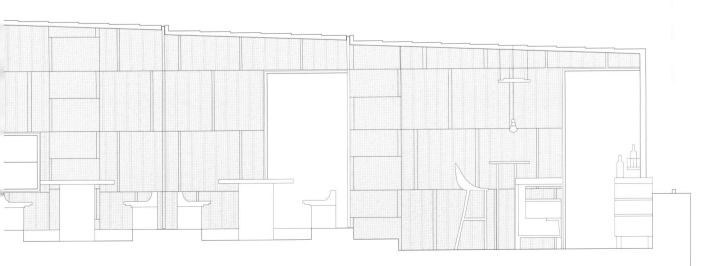

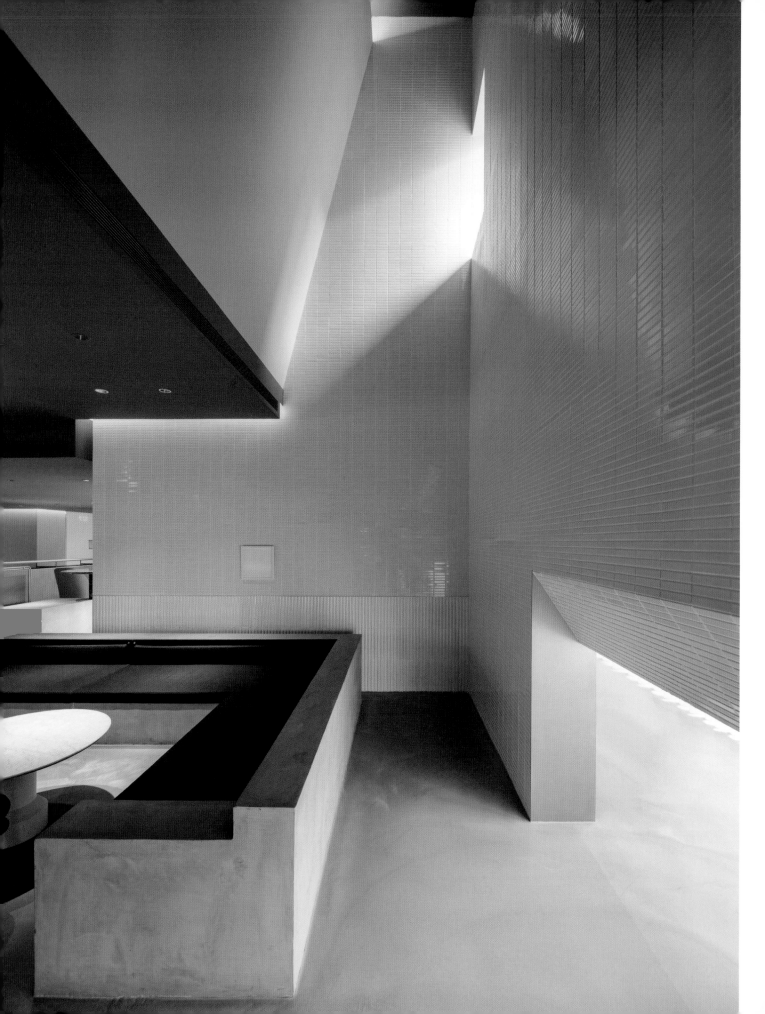

the urban sanctum
kimpton da an hotel

1

Located in the vibrant Da'an district of Taipei, Kimpton Da An Hotel is designed after the concept of an interior sanctuary – an urban retreat that offers a sense of calm and respite from the city's bustling streets and alleys, without losing the vibrancy and richness of its unique urban context. This guiding concept is reflected in every aspect of the project. The journey throughout the hotel is calibrated to remove visual distractions while emphasizing the passageways between programmes with expanded thresholds, accentuating each moment of encounter.

Guests begin their journey on the ground floor by entering the lobby, where they are immediately greeted by an intimately scaled reception lounge. The key element of the lobby design is an inserted carved mass, which allows natural light inside for a play of light and shadow to accentuate the space. The sculpted ceiling with varying depths offers different spatial experiences – a cocooned space for the lounge area and a double-height atrium upon arrival. The tiled walls with curated openings, which frame the garden outside and provide a quiet backdrop for the lounge, are a nod to the ubiquitous tilework found in the alleys of Taipei. Similarly, refined metalwork takes inspiration from the intricate layers of craftsmanship found in window and façade details in the surrounding neighbourhood.

The guestroom is the most intimate manifestation of the whole sanctuary concept. Wooden insertions, expressed as thresholds, divide up the room to create in-between spaces. Enclosed between thresholds, the guest is offered a momentary retreat – an introverted space for contemplation. Openings and windows are punctured and expressed as light-coloured wooden portals, offering internal vistas as well as views to the exterior. Since the project is a conversion of a residential building into a hotel, the design manoeuvres around the limitations imposed by the idiosyncrasies of the existing plan. To work with the variances of room types, bespoke wooden millwork elements are strategically tailored to create various functions for guests' needs. Windows and doors are then integrated into the wooden millwork to provide access to the balcony, revealing the view to the exterior.

In contrast to the guestroom experience, the restaurant is a celebration of communal dining as an extension of the rich street culture of Taipei. Different communal areas are divided by continuous enfilade walls, creating a series of interconnected spaces, referencing a common typology found in Asia. In elevation, the enfilade walls are lifted off the floor with wooden legs; in plan, they detach from the existing building perimeter, giving the walls a sense of ephemerality. The custom-designed wallpapers feature richly coloured, fluted tile and metalwork patterns inspired by the streets and alleys of Taipei. Each exploration within the hotel's spaces immerses the guests in a unique setting that provides a fresh ground for the contemplation of the relationship between contemporary travel and dwelling. The contrast offered by this urban sanctum provides an experiential rupture from prosaic everyday life, yet through abstracted motifs still evokes the lively context waiting just beyond its hermetic shell.

taipei

interior
products
branding
environmental graphics

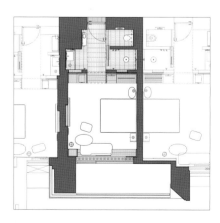

type a

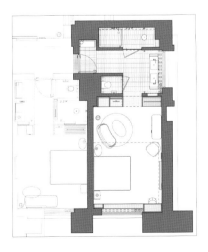

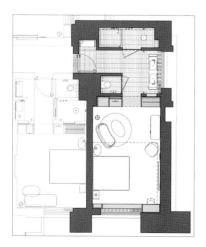

type c

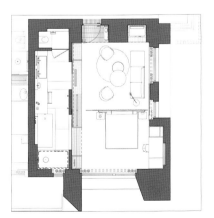

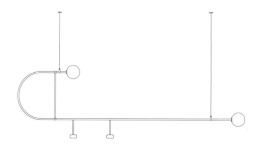

lobby light 1:50

restaurant light 1:50

 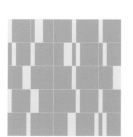

foyer bench 1:50

logo

wallpaper patterns

custom furniture l branding l environmental graphics

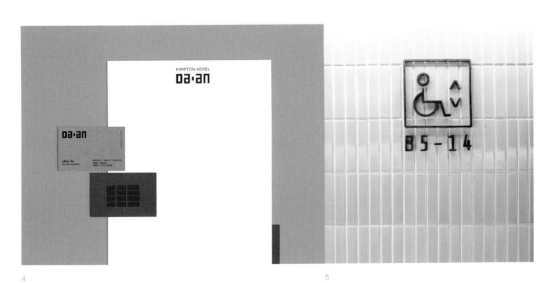

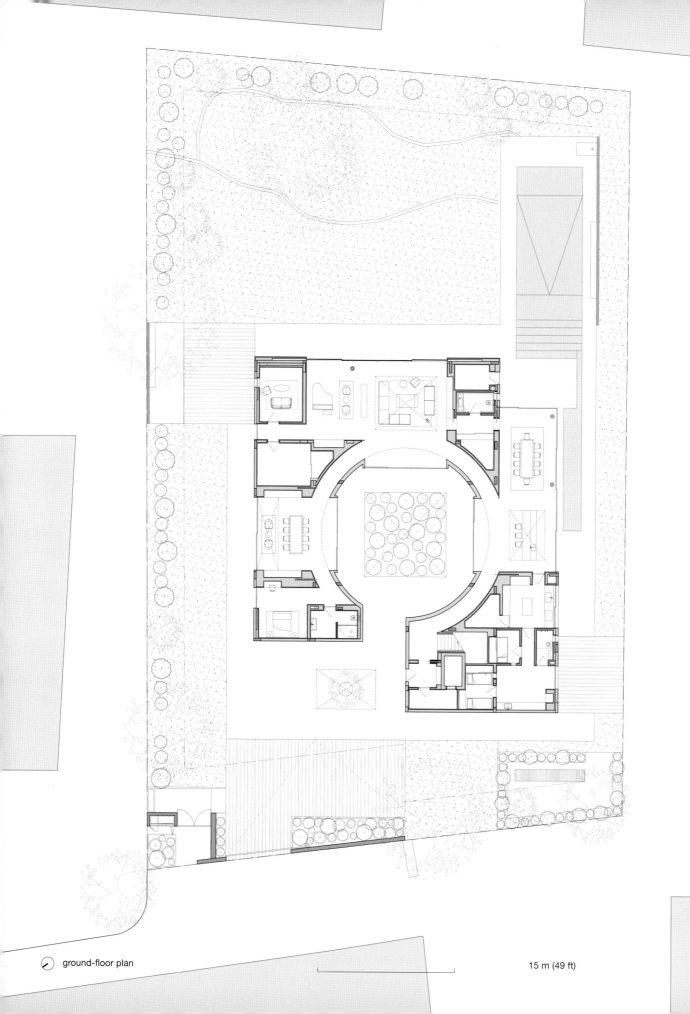

ground-floor plan

15 m (49 ft)

the house of remembrance
singapore residence

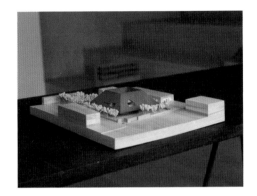

The traditional Chinese courtyard house, or *siheyuan*, is a typology well known for its illustration of Confucian ideals, accommodating extended family units whereby many generations live under one roof. To live under the same roof means to live together, and this metaphor is the nexus that ties the notion of community, especially in an intimate context, to the form crafted for this project. For this private residence commission, we were given a set of unique requests by the client: the new house constructed in place of the previous one should accommodate all three siblings, who as adults have outgrown their shared house; it should include a small memorial space in the form of a garden for their late mother; lastly, the new construction should retain the memory of the pitched-roof form, a defining feature of their childhood home. The previous house was built in the style of the British colonial bungalow, with hybrid elements of traditional Malay houses such as deep roof eaves for rain shelter, as well as Victorian details. Understanding the functional importance of the roof and the client's emotional attachment to its form, we embraced the symbolic nature of the pitched roof and combined it with a reinterpretation of the courtyard house.

In this project, we explore how notions of communal living and collective memory can be expressed spatially. The original site featured a lush vegetated edge that formed a natural green buffer along the perimeter, a feature that we have retained. The new two-storey house organizes all communal spaces around a central garden, which occupies the courtyard space serving as a memorial garden for the family's matriarch. The ground level is extroverted in nature, with expansive glass walls to connect all spaces to the gardens along the edge of the site. We aimed to maximize visual transparency from the communal areas – living room, open kitchen, dining room and study – so that from the ground floor the inhabitants may look into the central memorial garden while cocooned by the dense vegetation surrounding the house. Large glass doors can slide open, so that in optimal temperate conditions the house can take advantage of cross ventilation and direct access to the gardens.

For the upper level, we pursued the idea of the pitched-roof form not only as a signifier of shelter, but also as an element that both unifies and demarcates the public and private realms. All private bedrooms, located on the upper introverted level, are

housed within the roof's steep gables, so that when seen from the exterior, the house retains the appearance of a single-storey hipped-roof bungalow. Skylights and large glass walls connect to bedroom balconies where views are oriented outwards to the perimeter garden spaces. Through sectional interplay, we introduced three double-height areas to connect the communal functions and the corridors above. These spaces of interpenetration create vertical visual connections to allow one to peer into the public realm from the private.

One can see a carved void in the roof volume, which frames a small tree before arriving at the central memorial garden. On the exterior, where balconies and sky wells are carved out from the volume of the pitched-roof form, the walls transition from smooth to board-formed concrete to take on the texture of wooden planks. The circulation on the ground floor is based on the shape of the circle to reinforce the ambulatory experience of walking in the round and to define the memorial space as a sacred element. Since the circle has no edges or terminating vantage points, it allows one to always find a return to the centre both spiritually and physically. The garden symbolically defines the heart of the home as an ever-palpable void, persisting as the common backdrop to the collective lives of all inhabitants.

1

inhabitable strata

The dichotomies of architecture versus interior, outside versus inside are binary relationships we challenge through our work; these tropes, as Gaston Bachelard eloquently describes in *The Poetics of Space* (1958), merely reduce human experience to a geometrism that falls short of representing the full spectrum of inhabitation. Many of our projects demonstrate that we work with recurring themes of stereotomic massings, using carved voids to seemingly reinforce the notion of a figure-ground. At one end of the spectrum, we strive for legible forms that communicate permanence; yet conversely we defer to spatial plasticity to challenge readings of a singular narrative. The desire to embrace conflicting polarities stems from our complex attitude towards 'objecthood'. Although we gravitate towards heavier tectonic expressions that celebrate the weight and solidity that gravity offers as an allusion to permanence, after having established formal legibility, we interrogate the form from the interior.

Our projects' formal manipulations result from a process of working through a nuanced set of pressures related to the notion of poché (the black or filled-in parts of a plan representing solids, such as walls or columns). Robert Venturi and Louis Kahn reinterpreted the nineteenth-century concept of poché, elevating it from just recording the thickness of walls to a concept wherein the poché gives shape and character to space. For us, the notion of poché is not used to reinforce binaries, but as a means to unravel the oppositions of solid versus void and inside versus outside. From Venturi we understand poché as an index of the 'struggle' between pressures on the interior and exterior.[9] We constantly return to the poché's ability to give hierarchy and order while also accommodating differences and embracing tensions.

In Sculpted Light (p. 194), an aperture is introduced to the threshold between the pavement and entry to introduce dramatic foreplay into the experience of the theatregoer. Both the Library (p. 212) and An Enigma of Volume (p. 204) present a solid monolith, which is then eroded, excavated and interrogated from within as internal programmes begin to dictate organization. Predating these concepts of poché, we also take lessons from Gottfried Semper, who not only established the notion of the tectonic and the stereotomic, but more importantly decoupled architecture's origins from the erection of solid walls, and instead linked primitive construction to nonstructural woven textiles. If the wall as a point of exchange becomes the architectural event for Venturi,[10] in Semper's terms the nonstructural spatial divider holds even more potential to destabilize objecthood.[11] In the Lantern (p. 216), the poché diagram inverts to encapsulate what Venturi termed as *open poché* (open residual space), where the density of linear elements aggregates to take on a solid appearance – in which the definitions of wall, screen, canopy, line and volume are blurred to create a dense inhabitable stratum.

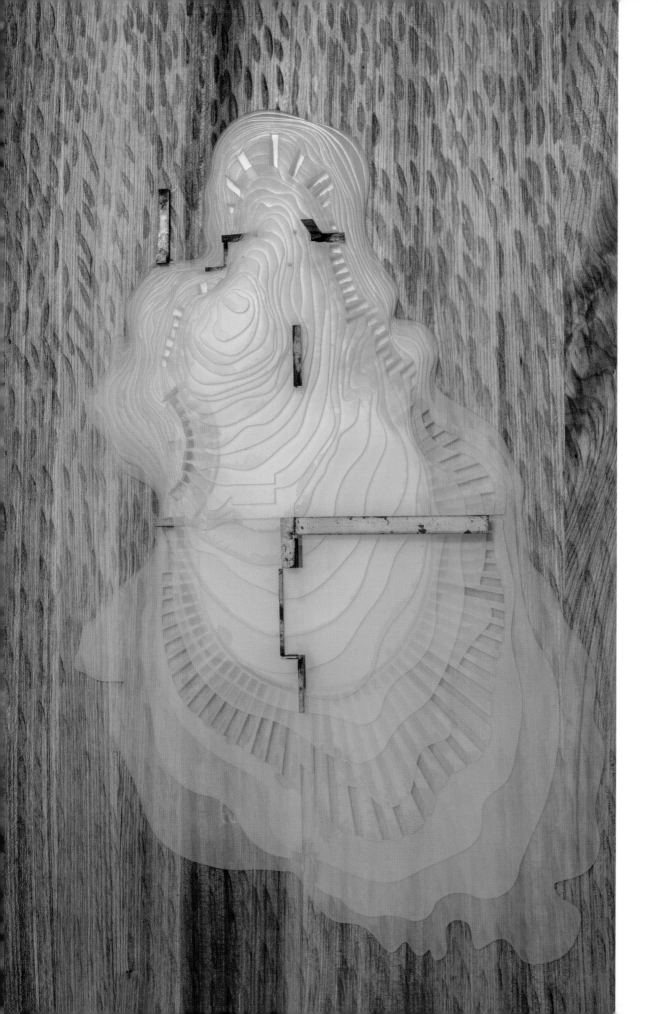

100 etchings: a journey within
14th venice biennale 2014

The word 'tour' derives from the Latin root *tornare* or Greek *tornos*, a lathe or circle, and when combined with the suffixes *-ist* or *-ism*, suggests the action of moving in a circle. A 'tourist', without the burden of prevailing commercial implications, literally and simply means 'one who moves in a circle'.

Inherent in the notion of circumambulation is the aspect of ritual. To journey in the round, where the beginning is also the end, is symbolic of an act fulfilled. The proposal here is to etch this metaphysical journey on to the physical site, wherein the concept of travelling is not contingent on actual destinations but rather describes an inner journey, a passage through space and time that results in a renewed understanding of oneself.

The basic unit of inhabitation here is both common and distinctive, just as is each individual inhabitant. Satisfying the basic functional needs of living, the plan configuration of each unit is identical, while the sectional quality of each room is determined by the specific topographic conditions and sun orientation at any given point, resulting in one hundred unique rooms. These units are linked with a continuous looping corridor, and cross-connected with a series of traversing tunnels. Public spaces are likewise sculpted into the ground, but on the surface of the terrain, exposed to the changing elements.

The primitive nature of the chosen tectonic of carving is reminiscent of a collective memory of space-making, found among ancient and contemporary cultures alike. Starting with the Greek approach to planning where buildings are firmly grounded in existing site conditions – demonstrated by the classic Greek theatre, which reacts to the morphology of the terrain, as well as Socrates' house, which reacts to light and air – and from these to the underground troglodyte dwellings of Tunisia, or the *yaodong* cave houses of China, the poetics of such spaces – etched into the earth itself – become grounds for a new kind of tourism.

Confronted with the questioning of a Greek identity in light of pervasive trends towards globalization, the position taken here is a full-circle return to the most primal means of inhabitation, and to an introspective journey of self-discovery.

venice

exhibition
graphic collaterals

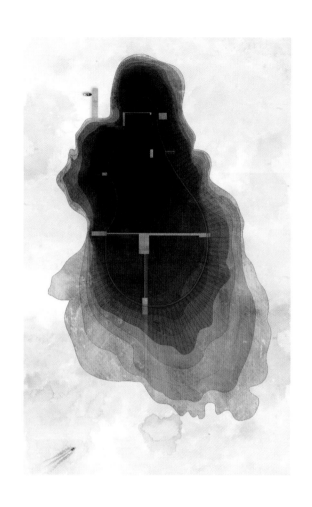

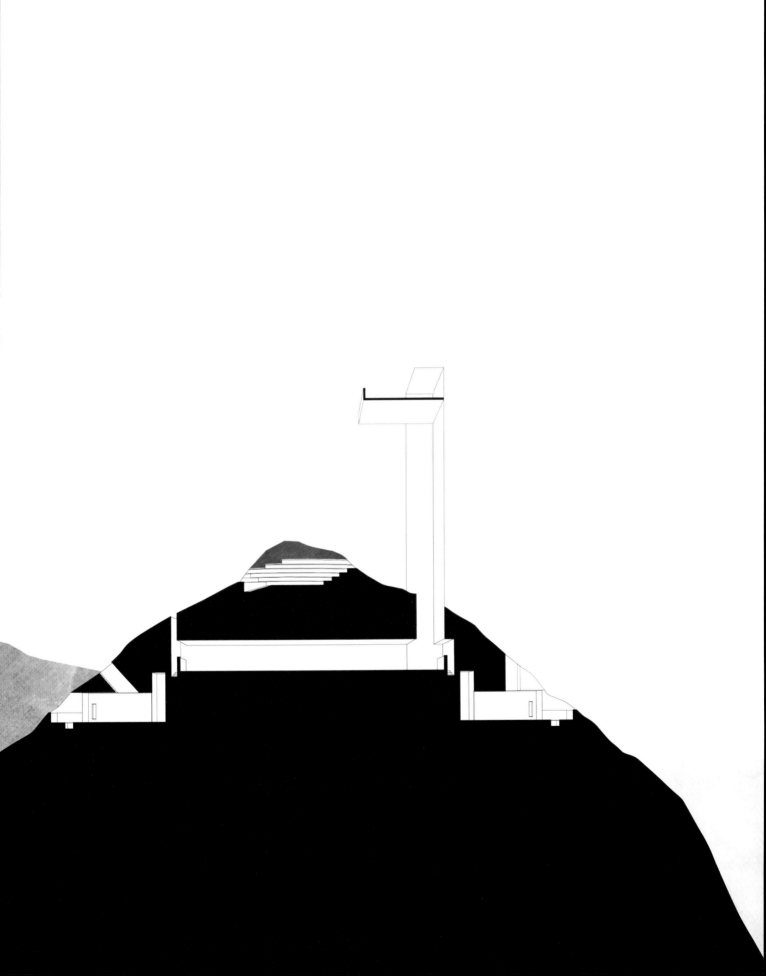

100 m (328 ft)

sculpted light
new shanghai theatre

1943

1990

2014

Occupying the site of a former theatre dating from the 1930s, the existing building, as we found it, had undergone a series of renovations over the decades, and much of the original character and architectural details had been stripped away. The resulting building was a pastiche of various styles and programmatic uses. Therefore, the primary design challenge was to recall the clarity and unity of the historical building in all its grandeur, creating a timeless architecture that would not only be relevant to contemporary life, but also have the potential to become a lasting and significant landmark for Shanghai.

From the street, the new building reads as a heavy stone volume hovering just above the ground level. The two upper floors, encased entirely in stone, relinquish any outwardly visible openings on the façade; instead, light and vistas are introduced via the vertically carved skylights. Drawing inspiration from the theatrical performances that take place within, the carved spaces of the interior and exterior atriums are conceptualized as a series of dramatic scenes. Varying spatial and lighting configurations are experienced as one moves throughout the space, intensifying as one explores deeper into the building. Several apertures take advantage of fluctuating light conditions throughout the day to create an ever-changing dynamic environment, while supplemental evening lighting mimics these conditions for added drama.

To guide theatregoers into the building, fluted bronze walls – reminiscent of a theatre curtain cloaking the drama on the main stage – provide a sense of weightlessness in contrast to the heaviness of the stone above. The entry and ticketing areas are recessed from the pedestrian walkway in order to create a covered plaza that is not only a shelter from the elements, but also a space accessible from the street, blurring the boundary of public and private. The public at large and any casual passers-by are thus permitted a glimpse and partial experience of the building's theatricality, with or without a ticket.

shanghai

architectural renovation
interior
products
branding
environmental graphics

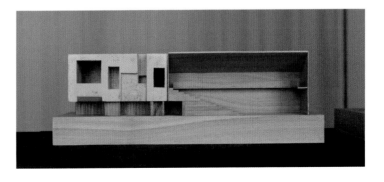

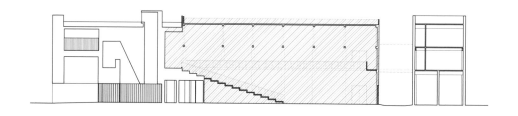

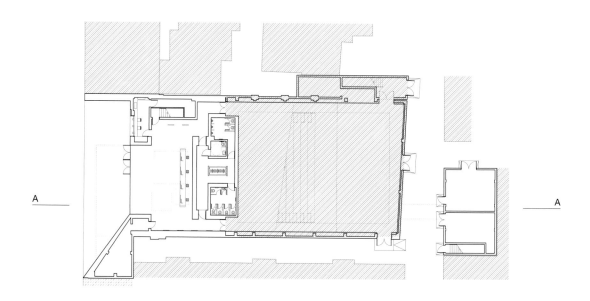

section | plan   20 m (65½ ft)

1 building threshold 2 pavement threshold 3 lobby skylight

4

5

6

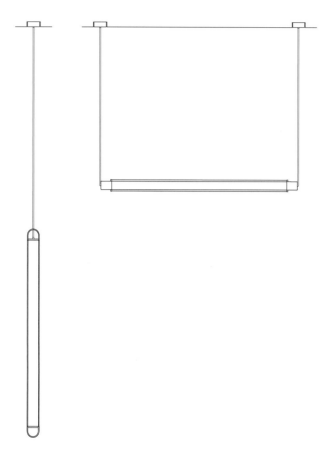

light 1:15

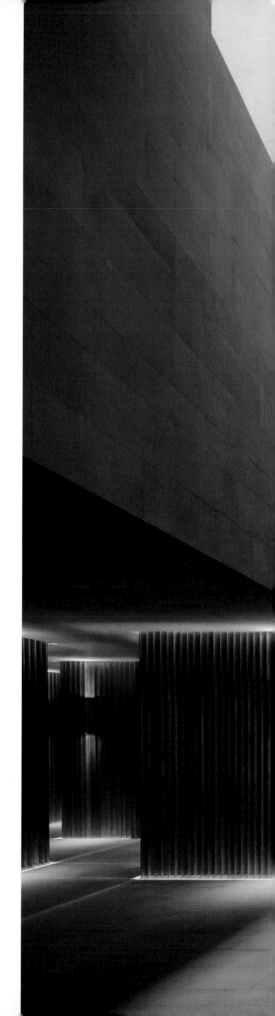

custom furniture

an enigma of volume
creative office in cologne

Ehrenfeld, a former industrial district in Cologne, now boasts a bustling multicultural arts scene. As a pivotal presence in the local creative industry with a vision to showcase a cross-disciplinary approach to design, our client decided to build a new office building next to its old one. The design eventually evolved into an assemblage of elements that organically take place within and around a monolithic concrete block, a presence whose inexplicable character reflects that of its environment and formation.

The only access to the building from the street is through a restaurant on the ground floor, while the main entrance to the office – which takes up much of the block's volume – is hidden from sight. The restaurant's vestibule opens up to a vertical void, revealing the meeting rooms and a library where visitors can catch a glimpse of the dramatic section upon entry. Another side of the block opens up to a courtyard via a series of operable screens that span the length of the building, allowing programmes to spill out to the surroundings. As one enters, the architectural object dramatically shifts to a progression of open, connected spaces – spaces that are seemingly 'unfinished' and 'useless' yet which invite spontaneous occupation and usage. The triple-height foyer is capped with a skylight and merges with a gallery, a photo studio and a restaurant at the opposite end.

The upper two floors house flexible open-plan office spaces. A main staircase serves as a promenade running parallel to the street, occupying the full height of the building and opening up via a skylight. Programmes inserted around the stairs lead to unexpected encounters as occupants of various floors intermix. A residential loft perches on top of the office building – a light structure of arches that provides living space for the client's family. The main space occupies the lower level, while an upper gallery is inserted as a place for work, rest and storage. In contrast to the heavier concrete mass of the office building, the loft's arches are fabricated from lighter concrete members, framing a space of air and sunlight.

One observes an interplay of solid and void as the building's enigmatic presence unfolds. The alchemy through which the disparate elements of this project – heavy walls, exterior appendage and interior vacuum – are bound together shows an act of space-studying with both tectonic and stereotomic methods. Curiosity is only heightened when a person enters a seemingly impenetrable object.

cologne

architecture
interior
products

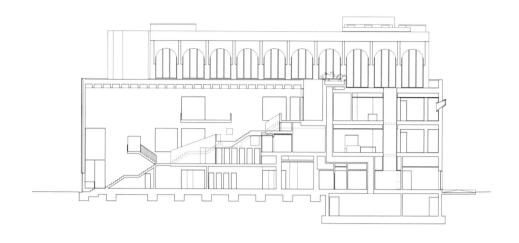

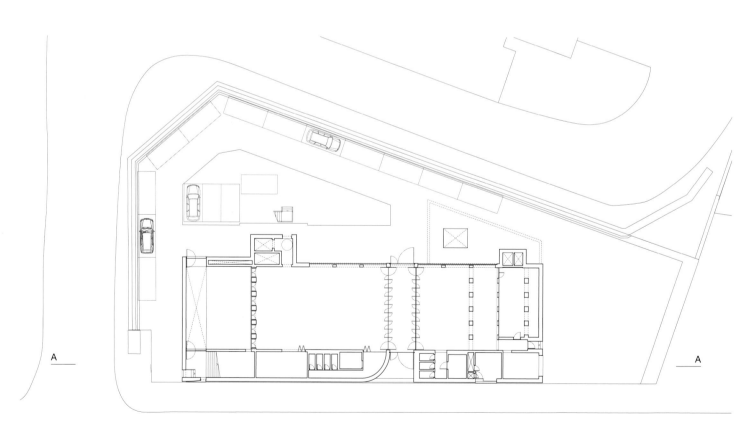

section ⏚ ground-floor plan   20 m (65½ ft)

1

2

3

4

5

6

the hub
performance and exhibition centre

Our design for a performance and exhibition centre in Hongqiao District, Shanghai, explores two contrasting building sensibilities expressed as a heavy stereotomic form (the *cave*) and a light tectonic structure (the *forest*). Stereotomics is an expression of the part of the building that yearns to belong to the compressive mass of the earth, while tectonics applies to that part which seeks to defy gravity and separate from the earth. According to Gottfried Semper, both structural expressions manifest human beings' desires to order and bind, cover and shelter that led them to create material assemblages. This project is a close study of how both categories of construction impulse – tectonics and stereotomics – may coexist to create a new type of corporeality in architecture.

A budding epicentre of culture and arts located upon a bustling transportation axis, the performance centre draws inspiration from primitive notions of shelter. The centre's interior is perceived as a five-storey urban landscape in the form of a solid rock, set inside an existing building envelope. Taking on the formal qualities of a cave, the walls are finished in grey sandstone, whose veins convey the accumulation of sedimentary layers. Visitors arriving from the metro station find themselves walking into a subterranean space, with the ceiling covered in suspended tubes, an allusion to the abstract metropolitan forest above. A dramatic escalator tunnel with deep ceiling coves brings visitors into the primary exhibition hall, experienced as a triple-storey clearing within the heavy stereotomic mass.

Lining the compressive stone walls, a dense filigree structure of wooden members is inserted as a floating canopy transforming the space into a large, interior forest. This secondary layer celebrates the tectonic articulation of joints, in contrast to the smooth and monolithic geometry of the cave. Set against the solemn walls of the cave, the tectonic forest comes into focus as a textured tapestry reflecting light, obscuring and revealing gallery spaces excavated beyond. Hidden above at the upper levels is the 'treasure box' – a large performance hall with floating wooden screens, referencing the bamboo slips from ancient China used to record the stories told within the space. The centre's interior landscape is a dynamic unity between the plasticity of the cave and the joining of discrete components – where line, surface and volume take form, ultimately presenting a comprehensive series of visual and sensory vocabularies.

shanghai

interior
products
environmental graphics

1

2

3

1 atrium 2 multifunction room 3 custom tile design 4 escalator ceiling feature

4

the library
valextra flagship store

The Valextra brand is known for its timeless leather goods that embody the balance between restraint and passion, an aesthetic rooted in its Milanese origins and core value of craftsmanship. The brand is noted for its innovative use of traditional materials to shape elegant silhouettes and unadorned forms through meticulous modelling of geometrical contours and folding constructions. Our design for its flagship store in downtown Chengdu plays on a similar concept of geometric sculpting, linking form together with function. Our design for the storefront, poised on a corner of a large development, takes the form of a rectilinear carved mass spanning two storeys in height and hovering uncannily off the street. To differentiate it from its generic shopping mall context, we conceived the façade as a solid concrete volume, a radical departure from the conventional retail glass façade. The mass levitates off the ground to produce a surreal moment of architectural tension, emphasized by the subtle lighting emanating from the interior.

The façade is composed of a series of geometric manipulations and deep vertical and horizontal cuts, which provoke curiosity in passers-by, teasing them with glimpses of activity within the space. Visitors cross the massive threshold through a carved vault that is geometrically off-centre, with part of its archway intentionally interrupted by the existing structure of the neighbouring storefront. Snippets into the interior are framed by the curved glass door, replete with details such as its brass handle and curved green tiles. Visitors are welcomed into the Library, an expansive circular space expressed in a material palette consisting of local reclaimed bricks, fluted white porcelain tiles and walnut wood. Bespoke wooden shelving is suspended from the ceiling to create a sense of enclosure and layering. This central space culminates in a display podium, where bricks rise from the floor to meet a slab of solid marble. Above, a deep conical light funnel painted in red illuminates the objects, infusing colour into the otherwise sober interior.

Nestled at the far back, the Reading Room returns to a rectilinear spatial format. This intimate space encloses both the products and the occupants with walls of curved green tiles, a material that imparts visual texture and depth by virtue of its reflective glazed finish. The brand's most exclusive products are presented in this introspective space, on a podium composed of richly juxtaposed materials. This culminating area conveys our dedication to crafted details, embodying the union of traditional crafts of materials and a modern, restrained aesthetic to create a retail experience that is identifiable with the brand, yet decidedly informed by its Chinese context.

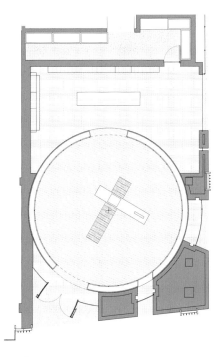

plan

A dialogue of geometric manipulations breaks down the interior volume into two connected spaces: the Library and the Reading Room. Located deep within the carved-out interior, the Reading Room is accessed through the curved wooden screen structure enclosing the Library.

chengdu

architectural renovation
interior
products

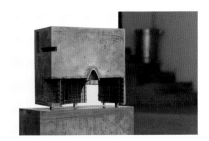

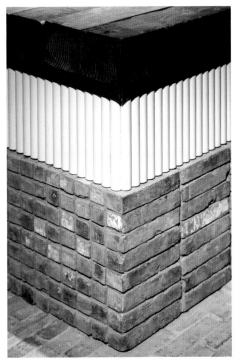

1 display podium detail 2 paving detail 3 arrival view

the lantern
sulwhasoo flagship store

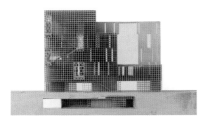

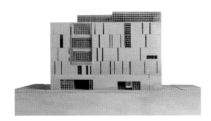

The literal and mythological meanings of the lantern are highly significant throughout Asian cultures and histories – it is an element that leads one through the dark, showing the way and indicating the beginning and end of a journey. Our transformation of an existing five-storey building in Seoul into a flagship store for Korean skincare brand Sulwhasoo was inspired by the lantern's symbolism. Sulwhasoo is notable for fusing modern science with ancient methods and medicinal herbs. To celebrate the roots of the brand, as well as referencing the search for beauty, the design concept aspires to create strong connections back to Asian heritage and traditions.

By sharing thoughts on the development of technology and objects in his essay 'In Praise of Shadows' (1933), Jun'ichiro Tanizaki depicts a culturally exclusive aesthetics shared within East Asia, particularly in China and Japan, that appreciates hazy and frail light – an indistinct mood playing on the edge between light and darkness, clarity and turbidity – as opposed to the full-bodied brightness often championed in Western cultures.[12] The lantern, often in the form of a candle enclosed by four walls of paper emanating soft light against a pitch-dark night, is an exact manifestation of this particular sensibility. It conveys a distinctively 'Asian' aesthetic. The concept originated from three key motifs – identity, journey and memory. The spaces are designed to appeal to all senses, capture visitors' attention immediately on approach to the building, create an experience that continues to unfold throughout the journey within, and leave a strong impression long after their departure. The final concept of the lantern is expressed as a continuous brass latticework – the unifying element that guides the visitors as they explore the full extent of the space.

A series of voids and openings was created in the existing building so that visitors are able to experience the intricate metal structure as it winds and extends through the space and encloses each distinct programme. Mirror-finish volumes are inserted into a wooden landscape to reflect and amplify the seemingly endless latticework. The delicate structure rests upon a solid ground of wide timber floorboards. The ground plane occasionally rises up to form wooden counters with inserted solid stone blocks, on top of which merchandise is displayed as precious objects. While it is primarily a guiding mechanism, the lantern structure is also a source of light – hanging within it are custom light fixtures and small mirrors that provide functionality to the armature, capturing the display of merchandise and the visitors' reflections.

As visitors move through the building, they experience shifts in the surrounding atmosphere. The basement spa, with its dark brick walls, earthy grey-stone treatment rooms, and warm-toned, crafted wood floors, offers a sense of intimacy and shelter. Moving up the building, the material palette becomes lighter and more open, inviting visitors to interact with the space. The vertical movement culminates in a roof terrace with a densely articulated brass canopy that frames vast views of the city. The journey is a constant contradiction between opposites: enclosed and open, dark and light, delicate and massive. The holistic approach to the lantern concept – from space-making to lighting to display to signage – provides an enduring atmosphere of endless intrigue and the search for beauty.

seoul

architectural renovation
interior
products
environmental graphics

1

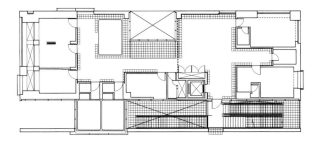

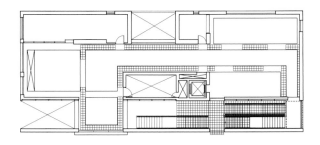

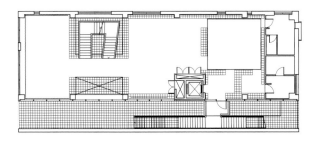

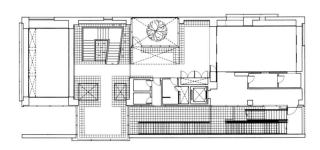

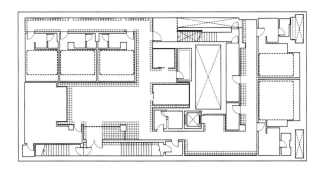

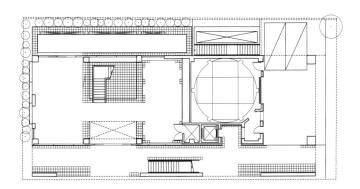

15 m (49 ft)

2

3

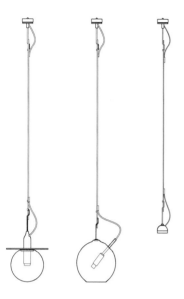

sul sole va for viabizzuno 1:20

In our everyday existence, light serves us by enhancing everything around it, while itself is often neglected. Here, the attention is given back to the source of light, treating it as an invaluably precious, albeit fragile element. With its delicate wiring and bulb exposed, it requires the additional armature and structural support of the leather strap and brass hooks, while the glass bulb cocoons and protects its gentle glow.

sedan chair for classicon 1:30

With its Sedan Chair, Neri&Hu completes its product family with a lightweight, elegant and comfortable chair. As is the case with the Sedan Lounge Chair, the special attraction of the design is the contrast between the seat shell and the frame: the seat shell visually wraps over the frame like a cover.

jie for nanimarquina 1:70

The Street carpet takes Chinese street and garden paving patterns and translates them into a multi-levelled and textured carpet.

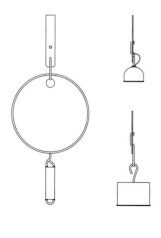

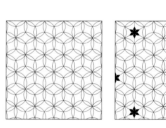

brass screen 1:50

mirror and weights 1:10

light 1:50

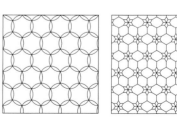

wood screen 1:50

4

5

6

7   8

a humble abode though this is, my virtues make it smell sweet. verdant are the stone steps overgrown with moss, and green seems the screen as the grass seen through it.

– liu yuxi, epigraph on my humble room (9th century CE)

recasting vernacular

To situate this next set of projects, we start with a series of questions. What is at stake for architecture today in relation to identity, where a globalized world and the digital age have radically altered the conventional notions of local versus global, centre versus periphery? What form can Critical Regionalism, a concept popularized by Kenneth Frampton, take in today's architecture, which diverges from an ethnocentric view of regional modern expressions as inherently working against the (imagined) core of Western hegemony? Is it possible to arrive at an architecture that is rooted in the particularities of place yet also transcends its locale to resonate universally?

We pose these questions because as our practice has evolved, the Chinese economy has seen a marked shift in developing inland provinces and rural hinterlands. As our projects have expanded in recent years from urban centres to the rural periphery in China, we have adapted our approach to finding modern expressions for an architecture that is contemporary and timeless at the same time, by virtue of its inseparable relationships to local specificity, materials and topography. In our practice we often examine vernacular typologies that have persisted for centuries in China, such as the *lilong*, *hutong*, *yaodong* cave dwellings, *tulou* circular dwellings and *chengqiang* walled cities. Like many architects practising in China who are exploring these typologies, we have found them to be critical in informing how we link new projects into a broader historical context, local lineage and specific site. Beyond typology, our recent investigations have also begun to look more closely at vernacular construction materials and methods. As with the approach to typology, we do not seek to transplant outdated modalities or take literal translations of a bygone element, but rather interpret them anew.

Although the essence of traditional construction in Chinese architecture is incredibly diverse depending on the province and region, we find the common thread to be the use of humble materials: stone, brick, concrete, earth, plaster and tiles. In several of our projects we have employed recycled bricks as a cladding material. Collected from demolition sites across China and reassembled in tactile patterns, these bricks are meant to gain a patina over time, giving the impression of having been there for many generations. This repurposing of reclaimed materials is not merely an act of sustainability, but also carries the idea of conserving time through curating the marks of history tectonically on a building's façade. In rural areas especially, the construction is extremely rough, yet out of the imprecision there is a certain beauty and simplicity that we choose to embrace. The whitewashed wall may not be as pristine as one would find in the Mediterranean, but in the wet climate of Jiangsu, it takes on soft greens and greys, like the brushstrokes of a Chinese ink painting.

   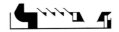

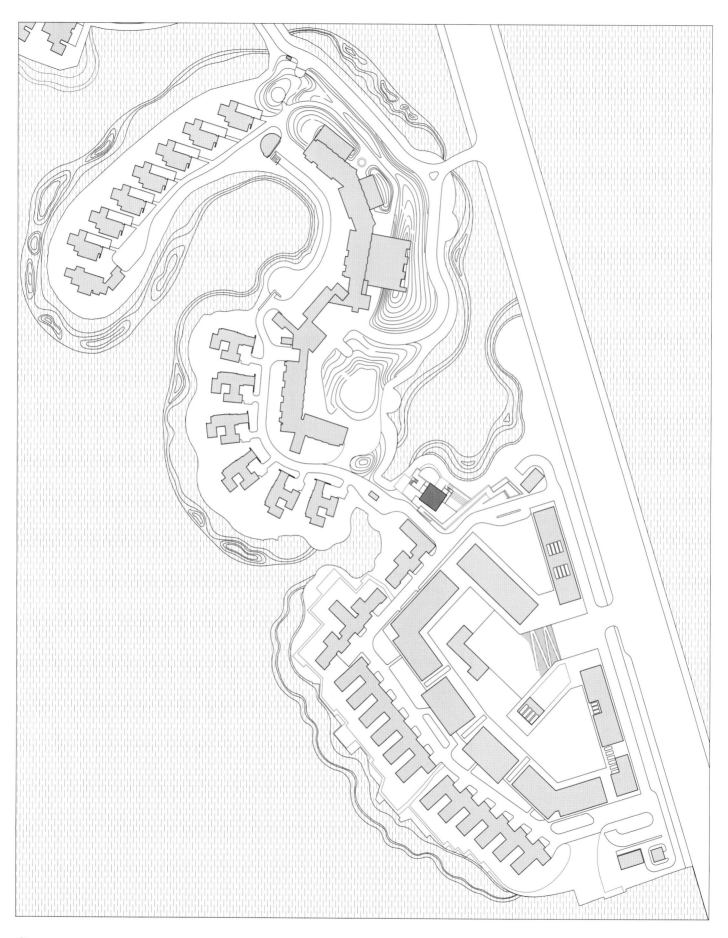

(1) site map

100 m (328 ft)

the sanctuary
suzhou chapel

Located along the scenic waterfront of Suzhou's Yangcheng Lake, the project sits at the heart of the Sangha residential and resort development, offering a spiritual haven for its community of local residents. More inclusive than a design for a particular religion or religious practice, the chapel is designed with the more universal notion of 'spirituality' at its core, a concept that can be understood by Eastern and Western cultures alike. Employing strategies from archetypical religious buildings – the controlled procession, the play of light and shadow, the contrast of spatial proportions, and the element of delight and surprise – the chapel provides the community with a place for quiet contemplation and refuge, as well as for lively gatherings and celebrations.

The design language of the chapel takes its cues from vernacular architecture of the Jiangnan region of China, which is notable for a soft palette of textured greys and whites. Brick walls of different heights are interwoven to compose a choreographed landscape guiding the visitor's journey. Collected from demolition sites across China, the recycled grey bricks continue the culture and history of the people, which is crucial for a building that is to be used as a core part of the community. Assembled in various bond patterns, the brick walls add a textured layer to the façade. Building up patina over time, the architecture begins to emerge as if it had been there for many generations, in a seamless integration with the surrounding landscape.

The white volume of the chapel perched atop is composed of two layers. The inner layer is a simple box punctuated on all sides with scattered windows, while the outer layer is a reticulated, perforated metal skin: a metaphorical veil that alternately hides and reveals. The double-layered façade creates a sense of mystery and spectacle for the building: during the daytime, it emits a subtle reflection under direct light, while at night it becomes a jewel-like beacon. Contained within the white box is the main chapel space, a light-filled, 12 m (39 ft)-high room with a mezzanine integrated into a wood-louvred cage element hanging above the space. A grid of glowing bulb lights and delicate bronze details give a touch of refinement to the otherwise austere monastic spaces. Custom wood furniture and crafted details complement the simple material palette of grey brick, terrazzo and concrete. A separate staircase alongside the main space gives unexpected views both internally and externally, as the visitor ascends to a rooftop deck offering unrivalled views across the lake.

suzhou

architecture
masterplan
interior
products

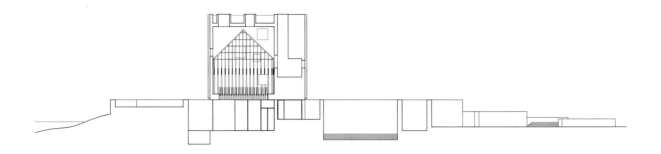

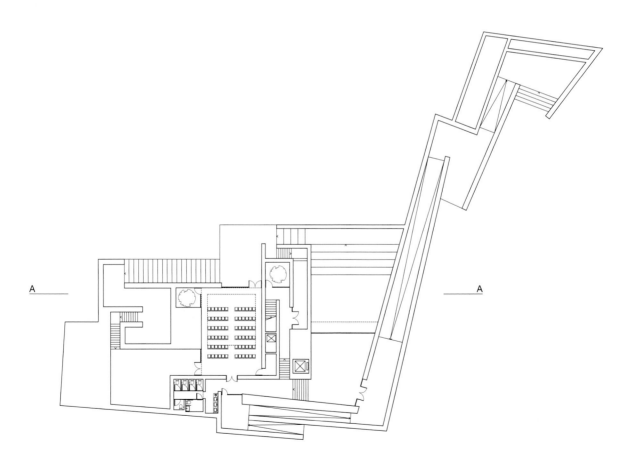

section l ground-floor plan

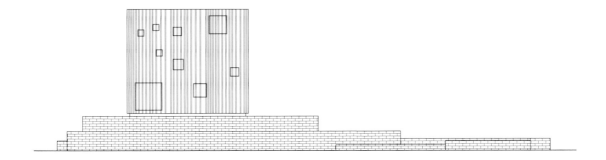

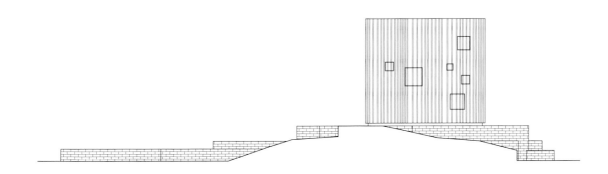

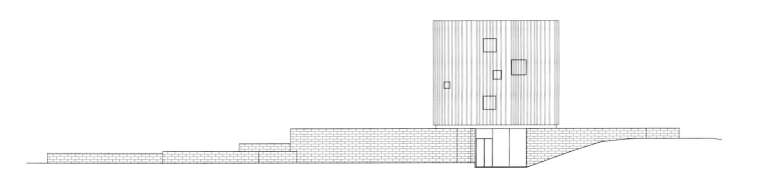

8 m (26¼ ft)

1

2

light 1:15

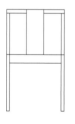

chair 1:30

long chair 1:30

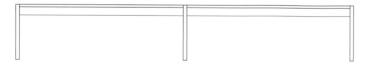

bench 1:30

custom furniture

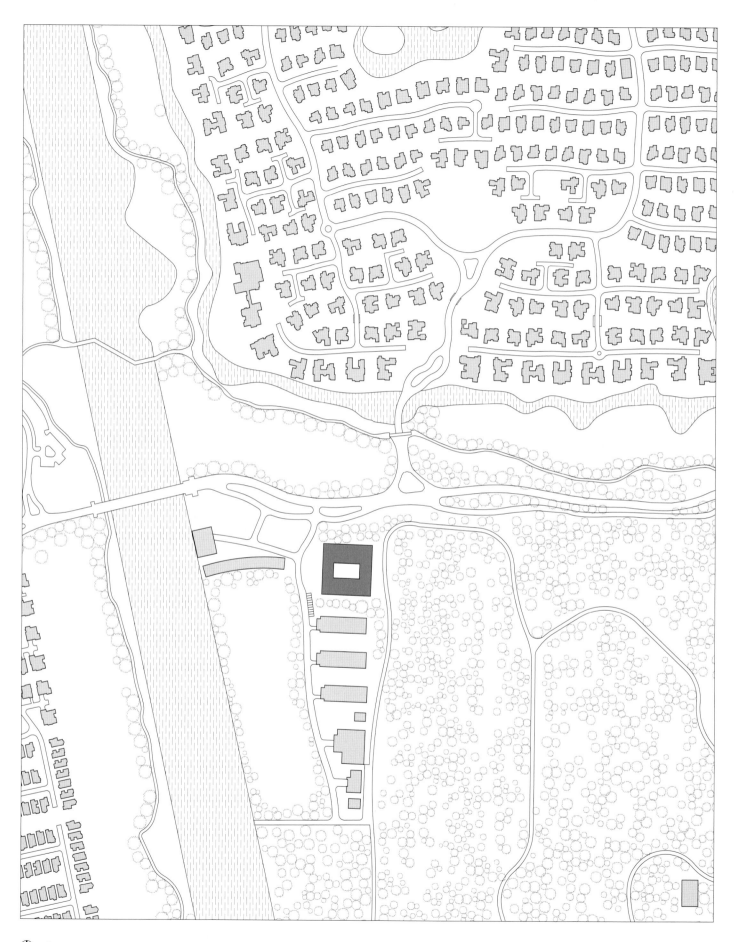

the interlocking journey
junshan cultural centre

1

Junshan Cultural Centre is located in the midst of undulating mountain ranges and meandering rivers near the Miyun Reservoir outside Beijing. The three-storey building serves the community of a private clubhouse and sales centre situated off the lush banks of the Bai River. The existing site was a doughnut-shaped, two-storey building adorned with neoclassical details – an architecture that felt incongruous with its lush natural surroundings. Drawing inspiration from the region's vernacular architecture, we grounded our scheme in the traditional courtyard typology and the heavy tectonic language belonging to northern China.

Our approach was to treat the existing building as a found artefact and transform it through selective deletions and grafted additions, balancing the preservation of the post-and-beam structure and the implementation of surgical alterations that would allow for spatial and programmatic experimentations. The building quietly rises out of the water as a screened brick mass with carved-out spaces for programmes, which are interlocked with gardens that form thresholds between the interior and the exterior. On the external façade, wood-patterned louvres, forming a continuous screen, are positioned at varying angles to create a light veil that softens the heaviness of the brick. Here, the brick plays a secondary role to accentuate shadow and relief. These louvres at the front are composed with different depths and angles, which produce shifting perceptions, giving the illusion of an ever-changing façade.

In the central courtyard, the brick mass takes on a dominant presence, and the ground plane is sunk one level to create more verticality to define an introverted space. We take advantage of the courtyard organization by crafting two sequences of interlocking journeys, one for community members and the other for visitors to the sales centre. Entering at ground level, a double-height reception hall welcomes all visitors before they embark on divergent paths to explore different public amenities. A recurrent aspect throughout the interior is the sculpted plaster ceiling: each space comes alive with unique geometric cuts carved out to interact with the sky. A primary feature of the centre is its library, formed by a series of bookshelf walls, which both provides intimate spaces for relaxing and reading and functions as an atrium space for hosting events. On the upper levels, the views are purposefully oriented back out to the uninterrupted vistas of the nearby mountain ranges.

Through the meticulous layering of the central courtyard, the small gardens, the brick volumes and the louvred screens, we were able to transform a lacklustre artefact into a place that resonates with its locale. Turning to nature as our guiding muse, we allow the building to merge harmoniously with the landscape to offer the community an enduring landmark intimately wedded to its context.

beijing

architectural renovation
interior
products
environmental graphics

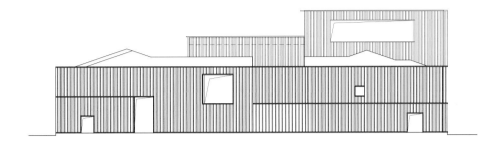

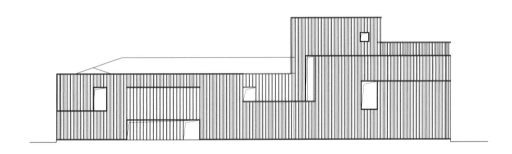

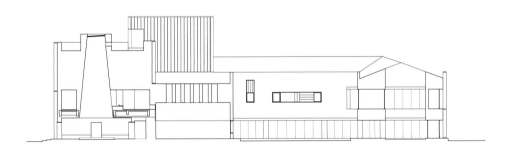

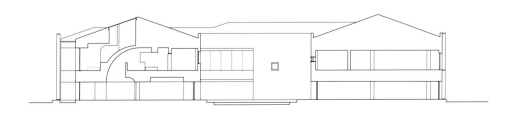

elevations I sections

20 m (65½ ft)

the relic shelter
fuzhou tea house

John Thomson, The Island Pagoda *(1871)*

Our project draws inspiration from imagery uniquely associated with Fuzhou: the Jinshan Temple. This is a rare example of a temple structure built in the middle of a river in China. John Thomson was one of the first photographers ever to travel to the country and provided Western audiences with some of the first glimpses into the Far East. In the album Foochow and the River Min, *which documented his legendary journey up the Min River, Thomson captured the ancient structure in its original state resting serenely above a floating rock in 1871. This would become a lasting image unmistakably identified with the city of Fuzhou.*

Conceived as an urban artefact and drawing from the historical roots of the city of Fuzhou, this project internalizes a piece of distinct heritage at a time when rapid new development has eroded traditional culture and identity. The client's brief posed the unique challenge of creating an enclosure for a Chinese artefact – the wooden residence of a high-ranking Qing dynasty official, replete with ornamental carvings and intricate joinery. Relocated from Anhui to its new home in Fuzhou, the Hui-style structure is enshrined as the inhabitable centrepiece of a new tea house.

Envisioned as a house atop a rock, the tea house is elevated above a rammed concrete base, while its sweeping copper roof echoes the roofline of the enclosed architectural relic. Its core material, rammed concrete, is a modern homage to the traditional earthen dwellings of the region, emphasizing a raw monumentality. Visitors are presented with two images of the building upon approach: the upright silhouette of the form, and its mirrored reflection duplicated in the surrounding pool of water.

A series of contrasts plays out among elements that are bright and dark, light and heavy, coarse and refined, as visitors enter the grand hall where the structure of the ancient residence is situated. Sky wells penetrate the roof, bringing natural light into the depths of the enclosure and illuminating the priceless artefact on display. Only upon reaching the mezzanine does the structural configuration of the building begin to reveal itself. The hovering metal roof is lifted 50 cm (20 in.) off the solid base by copper-clad trusses to introduce a sliver of continuous illumination around its periphery. Wrapping itself around the historical wooden structure, the mezzanine space allows visitors to appreciate intricate carpentry details at eye level.

The basement level includes a secondary arrival lobby housing a rotunda, a sunken courtyard and tasting rooms. At the top of the rotunda, a carved oculus capped by glass is submerged beneath the pool in the courtyard above. It filters the sun through a thin film of water, creating a mesmerizing play of reflections.

fuzhou

architecture
interior
products
environmental graphics

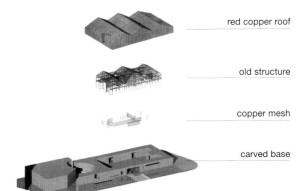

red copper roof

old structure

copper mesh

carved base

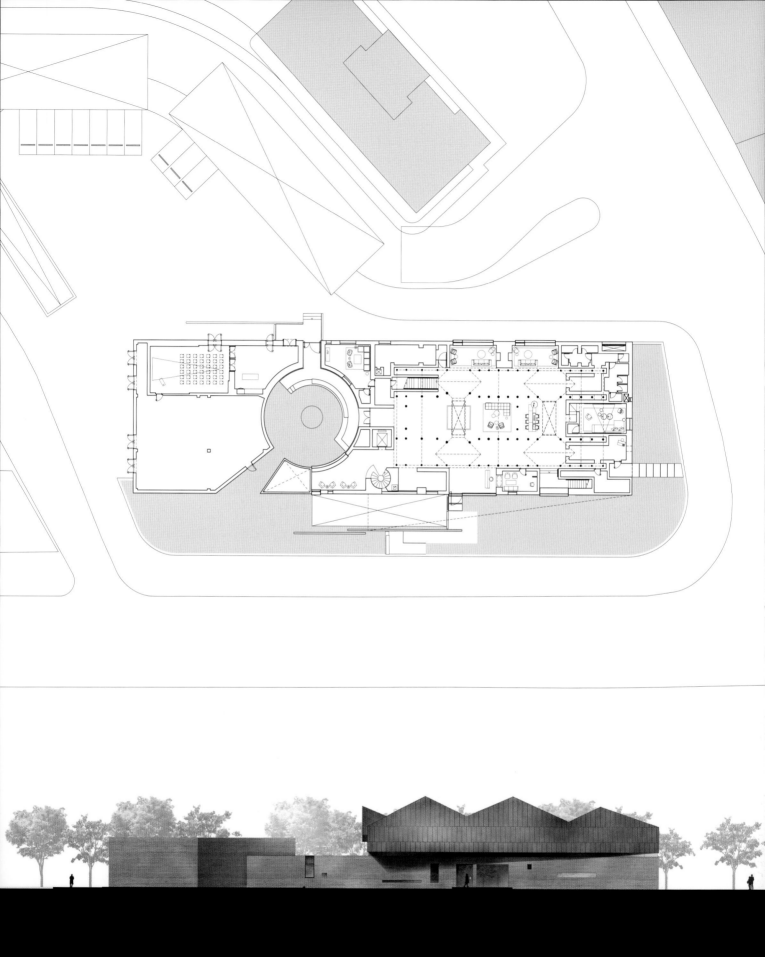

1

2

the ancestral hall
aranya museum of family history

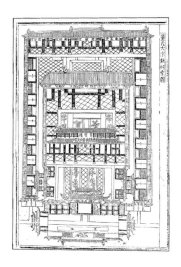

Liu Dan, plan of the Focal Ancestral Hall (built in 1562)

The ancestral hall, a common Chinese building typology, used to play an important role in village life and society. Many villages were formed by extended families sharing a surname, with a traceable lineage through multiple generations. While fulfilling certain functional needs of the village – such as a venue for weddings, funerals and other rites, and a place for educating youth and even for the settling of disputes – the ancestral hall symbolized the strength of the lineage and the bond between all village members.

It is often said that Chinese culture stems from rural roots. Yet as China's cities continue to grow at unprecedented speeds, its rural villages suffer the opposite fate thanks to urban migration. Once the villages disappear, so does the Chinese culture. Aranya's brief to design a contemporary ancestral hall in the rural mountains outside Beijing was a fitting opportunity to address this crisis. The idea of a modern ancestral hall aims to re-establish a sense of unity and solidarity, and to counteract the experience of displacement and rootlessness of an increasing migrant population.

To ground this project in a broader historical and cultural context, key components of the ancestral hall typology were first identified – the symmetrical plan, the sequence of public to private thresholds, and the void spaces at the courtyards. While remaining true to the floor plan of the vernacular typology, our reinterpretation brings innovation in section as well as in material and construction. A concrete post-and-beam structure forms the overall framework, while the wall infills consist of locally harvested rock built up with traditional masonry techniques. Juxtaposed side by side, the smoothness of poured concrete accentuates the rough texture of the stone walls. The robustness of modern concrete construction also allows for spatial breakthroughs – the dramatic clear spans. Here, concrete is not limited to merely a structural role, but at times takes on a sculptural one as well – it is carved out to create staircases, cantilevered balconies and tilted planes bringing in light. The tectonic simplicity of the building façade is enhanced by these unexpected mutations, which give the architecture a sense of playfulness as well as austerity.

A landscape journey brings people from the main residential villa areas to the hall, which is situated in the wetland valley between two mountains. Contrary to the typical ancestral hall, the approach to which is frontal, the unique site conditions dictate that the building must be oriented lengthwise along the mountain and accessed through a small side entry. Passing through this humble threshold, the visitor has to immediately adjust their orientation to be perpendicular and centred to face the first courtyard. Open to the sky, a traditional tiled roof slopes down low on all four sides of the square, a forecourt to the main interior space of the grand exhibition hall. Continuous colonnaded corridors flank both sides and extend the full length of the building, connecting with the two staircases, one at each end. A sweeping concrete curve is found in the final room of the building, dedicated to no particular function but simply a space for quiet reflection, for contemplating the common ground we share with all those who came before us.

jinshanling

architecture
interior

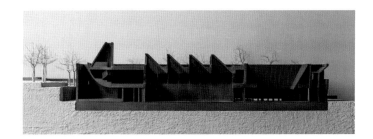

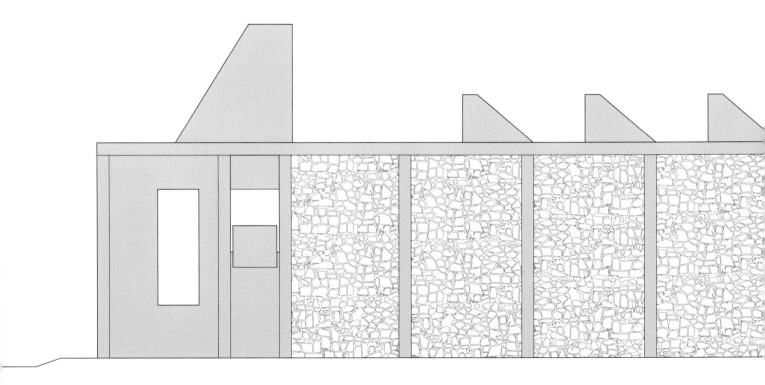

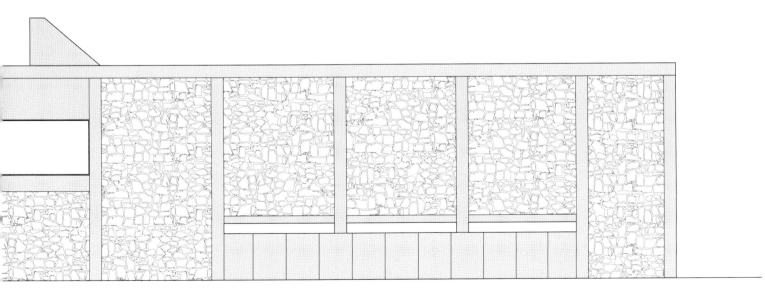

elevation

5 m (16½ ft)

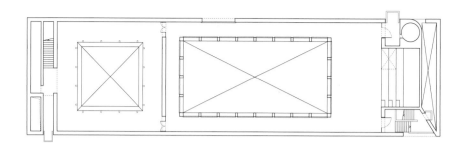

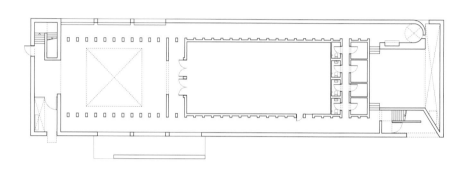

1

3

2

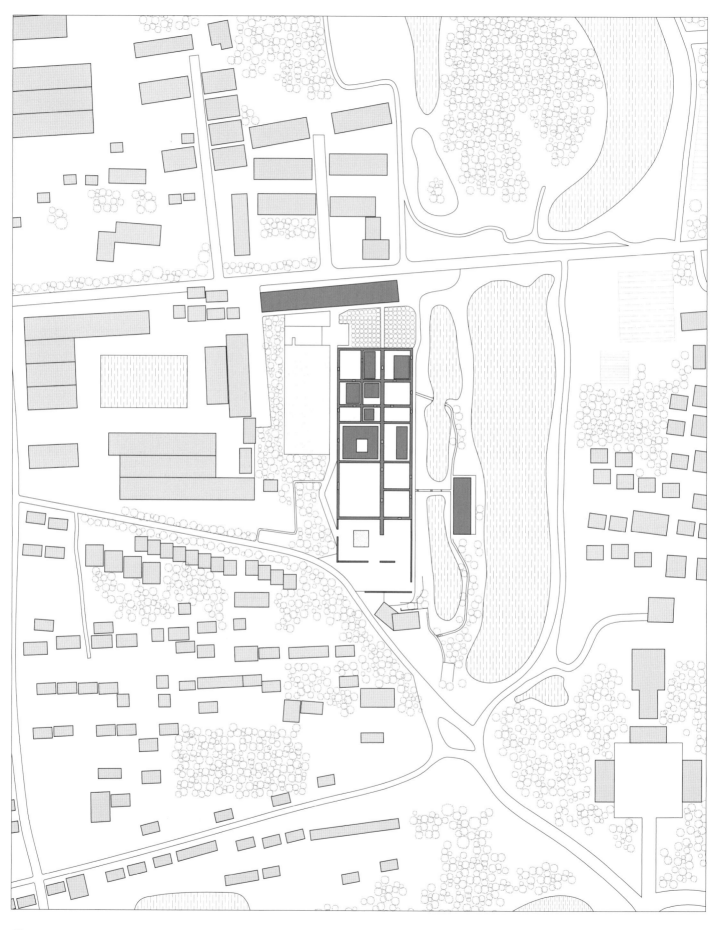

the brick wall
tsingpu yangzhou retreat

Inspiration from Chinese traditional gardens

Geyuan, one of the most notable gardens in China, created by a nineteenth-century salt merchant, is located in the northeast section of the historic city of Yangzhou. The layout of the garden complex adopts a typology that has a 'front house' (residential area) and a backyard. The southern residential building cluster adopts the layout of a 'nine palace grid' and encloses the construction with buildings. The two perpendicular axes form its main traffic thoroughfares and strengthen the physical connection between various courtyards.

Situated in close proximity to Yangzhou's scenic Slender West Lake, the site given to us to design a twenty-room boutique hotel presented a unique set of constraints. Addressing a site dotted with small lakes and a handful of existing structures, the design brief called for the adaptive reuse of several old buildings to house new functions, while adding new buildings to accommodate the hotel's capacity needs. In an attempt to unify these scattered elements, we overlaid a grid of walls and paths on to the site in order to tie the entire project together. The resulting organization creates multiple courtyard enclosures, a modern reinterpretation of the courtyard house typology in vernacular Chinese architecture. Like the traditional version, the courtyard here brings hierarchy to the spaces, frames views of the sky and earth, encapsulates landscape into architecture, and creates an overlap between interior and exterior.

Constructed entirely with reclaimed grey brick, the narrow interior passageway inside the gridded walls forces a far-reaching perspective, while light plays off the various brick patterns, enticing hotel guests to venture ever deeper into the project. Within the walls, several of the courtyards are occupied as guest rooms and shared amenities such as hotel reception, library and restaurant. Many rooflines of the buildings are confined within the height of the walls surrounding them, so that they are not visible from afar. Guests traverse the site using the walled pathways to discover their rooms. Once inside, there is a clear separation between the building and the walls, giving a layer of privacy and a sliver of landscape for guests to enjoy. Other courtyards are left unoccupied, serving as pockets of lush garden to offer relief from the sense of enclosure imparted by the brick passageways.

Journeying along the walls, guests can ascend through the openings above to gain privileged vantage points looking out across the gridded landscape and the surrounding lakes beyond. Here, three additional buildings show up in the panorama: the rising second floor of the largest courtyard building, a lakeside pavilion of four guest rooms, and a multifunctional building at the furthest reach of the site. An existing derelict warehouse building retrofitted with a new concrete structure, this multifunctional building houses a restaurant, a theatre and an exhibition space.

Our ambition lies in the strong utilization of the landscape element – the walls and courtyards – to unify the complex site and programmes, while the rustic materiality and layered spaces seek to redefine tradition with a modern architectural language. The essence of the project is most viscerally experienced in one of the courtyards connected to the reception space – sunk half a metre below ground level, the datum gives visitors the feeling of partial submersion into the surrounding expanse of still water. With its reflections of the fortified brick enclosure on the water surface, the ground plane is dematerialized, melding ground and sky, and merging human and nature into one.

yangzhou

architecture
masterplan
interior
products
environmental graphics

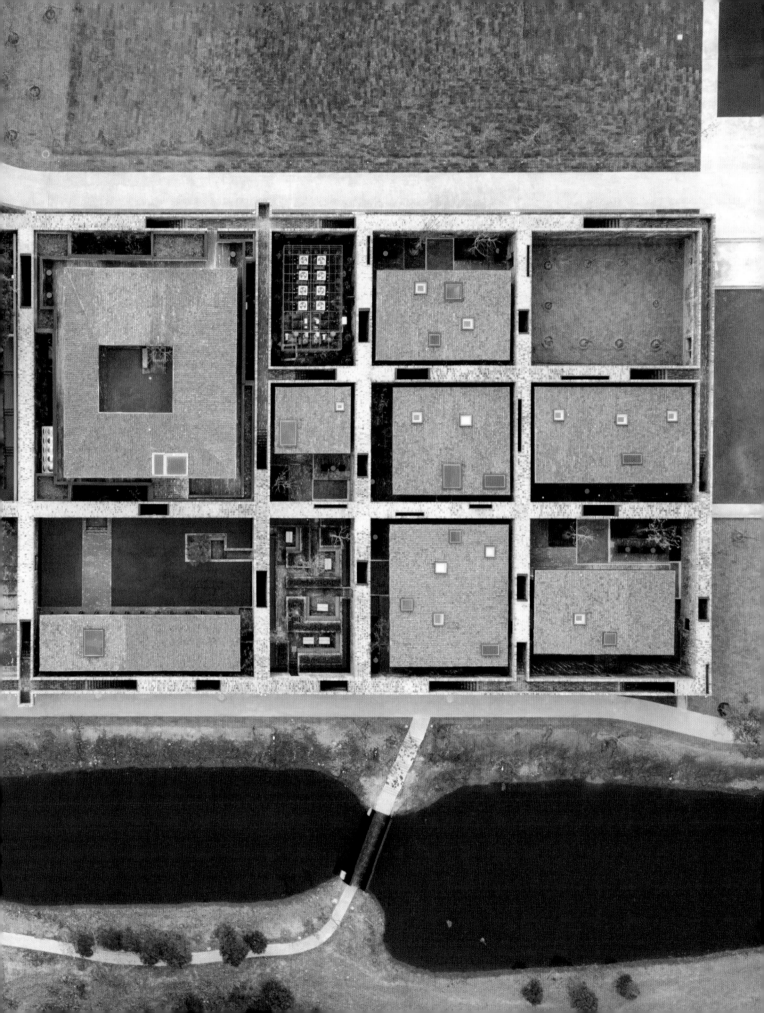

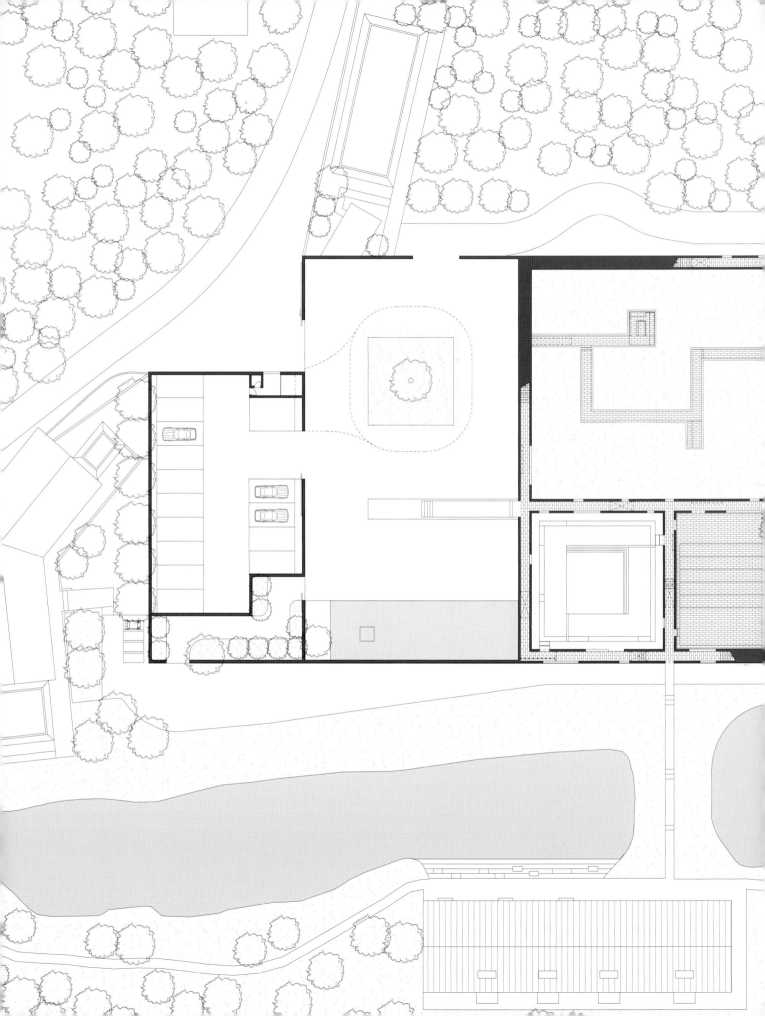

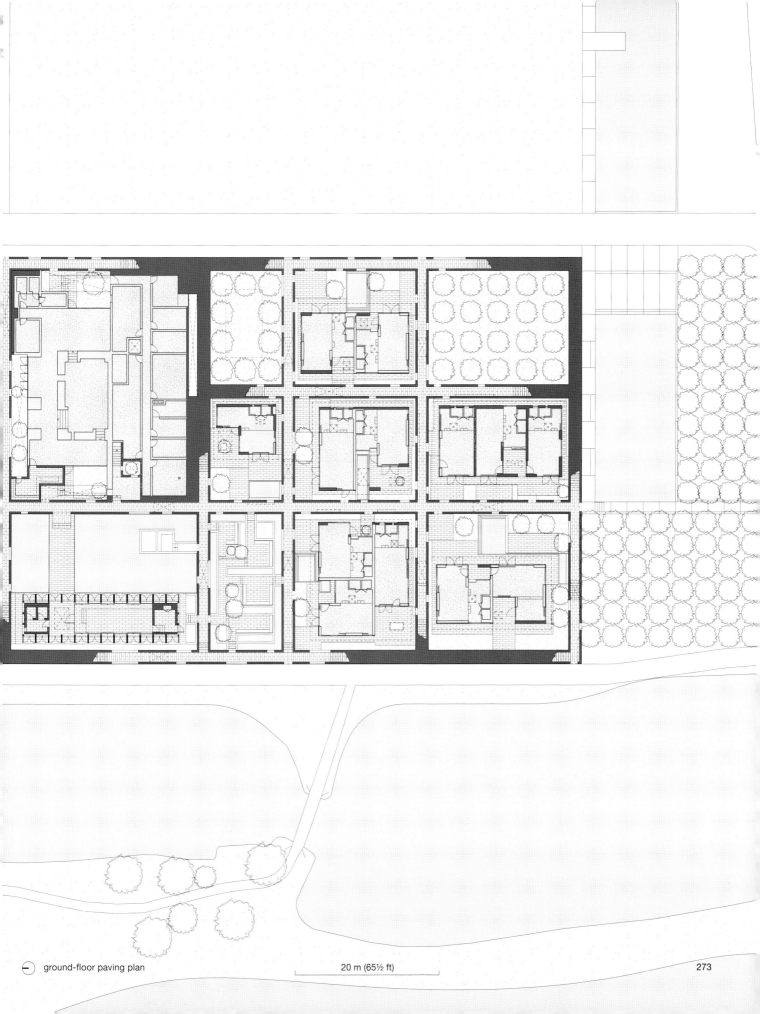

ground-floor paving plan

20 m (65½ ft)

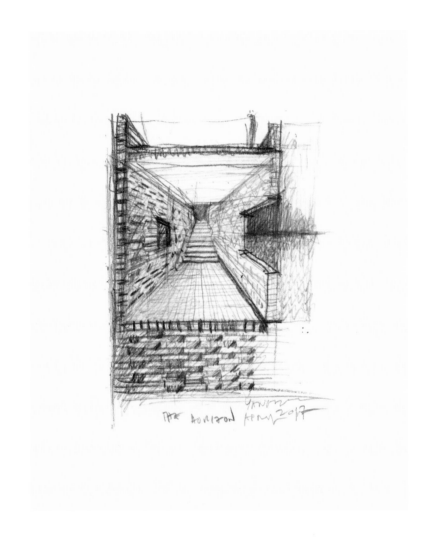

THE HORIZON APRIL 2017

1

2

3

4

5

6

7

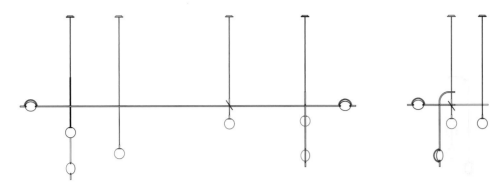

ceiling light 1:30

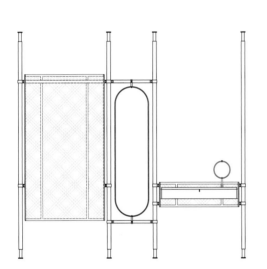

screen & mirror 1:40

wall light 1:15

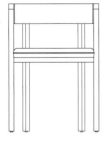

dining chair 1:20

stool 1:20

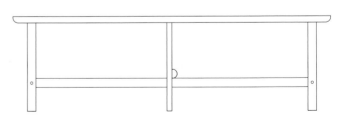

coffee table 1:20

future artefact

on top of the phoenix terrace
phoenixes used to roam,
now gone are phoenixes,
a desolate lookout remains
as the river continues to flow.
flowers and verdure of the
wu palace are now buried
under isolated trails,
the upper ranks and decorated
officers of jin are now mounds
topped with growth.

the barely discernible
trident peaks range
beyond the blue skies,
the river waters part into
two waterways that around
the egret islet roll.
floating clouds eventually
the sun conceal,
not seeing chang'an has me
worried in shadow.

– li bai,
atop the phoenix
lookout of jinling
(8th century CE)

We began this monograph with a chapter dedicated to 'reflective nostalgia', focusing on projects that adapt found artefacts seen as fragments in time, and imparting new life through design interventions. In this last chapter dedicated to our architectural works, we circle back to the temporal continuum connecting our present moment to the past, but shift the lens to contemplate the future. The notion of the monument and the conceptual framework presented in this chapter builds on the theories of architect Aldo Rossi, who conceived the city as a living entity, constantly transforming and accumulating its own consciousness and memory. Rossi argued that architecture's value resides within the forms of urban artefacts, which continue to structure the city even after they have shed their functions. It is not a question of if, but when today's newly erected buildings will become another architect's found ruin. The question we raise is simple: how do we create built artefacts that can retain a meaningful presence for generations to come? The following pages present a series of projects that have challenged us in how we deal with notions of context, the role of the monument, and the duality of destruction and evolution.

Our engagement with the Chinese context obliges us to expand Rossi's theoretical framework not only to the realities of the contemporary urban condition, but also to rural contexts. The challenge is to find and define 'context' in places where the built heritage is either disappearing, the surrounding fabric is newly constructed, or in some cases a *tabula rasa* is anxiously awaiting development. The term 'willing' in Chinese is composed of a juxtaposition of two characters, the first meaning 'to shed' and the second 'to receive.' This simple term points to a paradoxical sentiment that equally yields to both erasure and progress. The term 'creative destruction', a theory originated by economist Joseph Schumpeter, has been used to describe the condition of modern Chinese cities where the prevalence of demolition operates alongside rapid development.[13] While the wide acceptance of erasure as a means of urban advancement may seem odd, this attitude stems from a particular cultural relationship to history, both actual and conjectural.

To understand this attitude, we turn our gaze to the Chinese ruin. Unlike European buildings, ancient Chinese structures were often constructed out of wood, leaving behind only their foundations as traces of their original grandeur. As is evident in its etymology, the word for *ruin*, which evolved from the word *qiu* (connoting a mound of rubble) to *xu* (a signifier of emptiness), indicates that over time the concept of the architectural ruin was increasingly freed from external visual signs, relying on allusion rather than direct, literal representations.[14] In the works presented in this chapter, we aim to embody the essence of an ancient tree, historically associated with decay but also with continuation, persisting 'in permanent evolution, open to the dialectic of remembering and forgetting',[15] yearning to write its own anticipated fate.

the void
aranya art centre

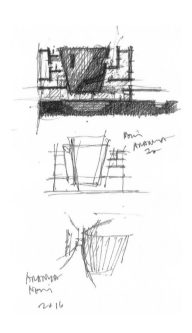

When enlightened developer Aranya asked us to design an art centre inside their seaside resort community located in the northern port city of Qinghuangdao, we were faced with a dilemma in terms of how to extrapolate from the immediate site context. Nestled in a new community not far from the coast of the Bohai Sea, the site's adjacent urban fabric is best described as that of a faux Mediterranean-style development. This sort of Disneyfication is not uncommon in China, so the question we posed to ourselves was how to create an architecture that responded to the brief, related to the locale, yet offered an alternative vision for the community's future. Fortunately, the client wanted something timeless, and challenged us to create an icon that would be true and representative of the Qinghuangdao region, which takes pride in its seasonality and access to nature. Working with the notion of *genius loci*, or 'spirit of place', we returned to geography, climate, light and tectonic form as the elements to engage with to create a dialogue with the environment at large. Drawing inspiration from the seasonal ocean waters nearby, our design for the building attempts to encapsulate the natural wonder of water at its core.

To translate the Aranya community's ethos based on an emphasis of oneness with the environment, we proposed a design scheme that is as much about an internal courtyard, a communal space for residents, as it is about the ancillary exhibition spaces. Despite the straightforward brief of an art centre, we seized the opportunity to question the notion of an art space versus a communal space. The building takes on a simple geometric massing that maximizes the structure's footprint to impart a decidedly heavy, elemental presence. Although visually imposing in contrast to its fabric, the art centre's formal language is a nod to the heavier tectonic forms of architecture in northern China. The fortress-like exterior conceals a central void space that can be reconfigured to function in many ways: a pool feature when filled with water, but also a performance and gathering platform when drained.

Within the thick mass of the building volume is a series of interlocking spaces that visitors can meander freely within, where they can slowly ascend with directed views both inward and outward. A spiralling promenade leads the visitor through each programmatic space, urging them onwards with a desire to see more. Starting at the base with the café, multi-purpose gallery and an outdoor amphitheatre, the path guides visitors through five distinct galleries, culminating at the rooftop for panoramic views of the activities below.

Composed primarily of various textured concretes, the façade articulation and the materiality of the building are heavy in nature, so that it may be likened to a solid rock sitting firmly in the shifting environment. Smooth surfaces reflect the changing skies, while the moulded modular units of the exterior walls create a play of shadows throughout the day. Bronze elements act as accents on the heavy façade, catching light and drawing attention to the entry of each gallery. Custom lighting and details add a touch of intricacy to the otherwise modest palette. In the evening, the building is transformed as light emanates from within, turning the solid sculpture into a glimmering jewel.

qinghuangdao

architecture
interior
products

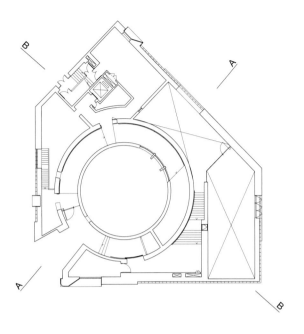

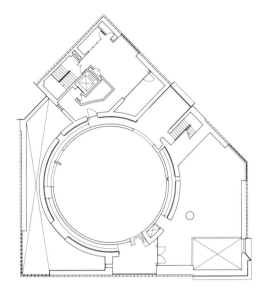

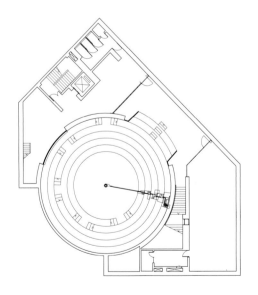

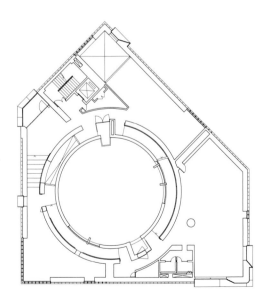

20 m (65½ ft)

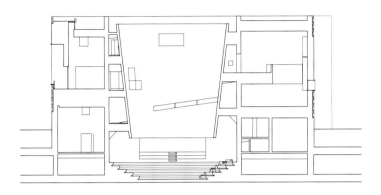

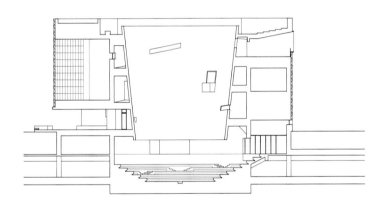

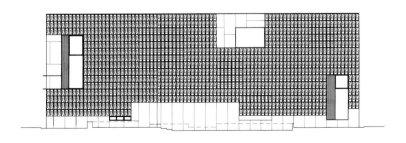

sections | south elevation

20 m (65½ ft)

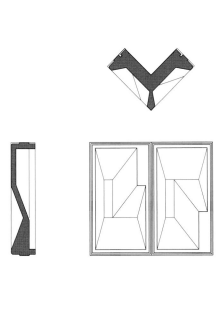

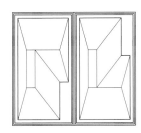

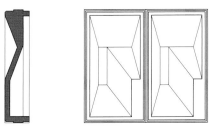

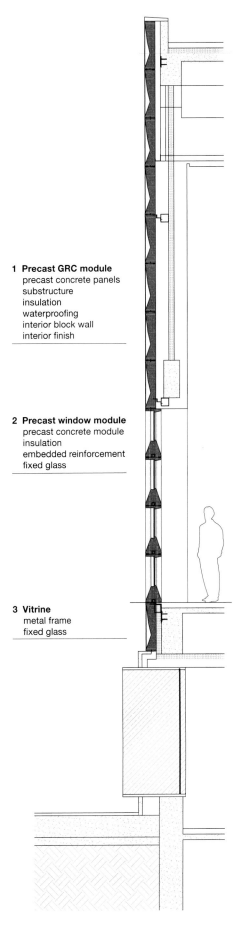

1 Precast GRC module
precast concrete panels
substructure
insulation
waterproofing
interior block wall
interior finish

2 Precast window module
precast concrete module
insulation
embedded reinforcement
fixed glass

3 Vitrine
metal frame
fixed glass

wall details   1 m (3¼ ft)   façade details   3 m (10 ft)

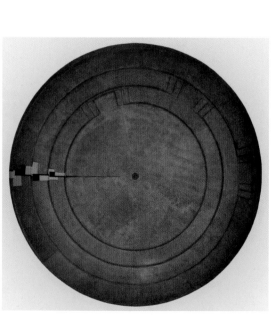

aerial view

1

2

3

4

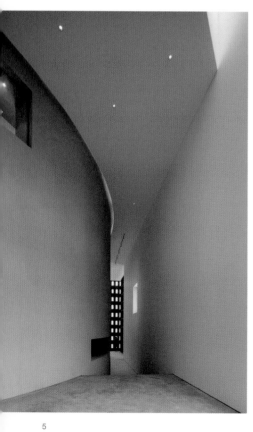

5

3/4 spiral ramp **5** gallery **6** atrium

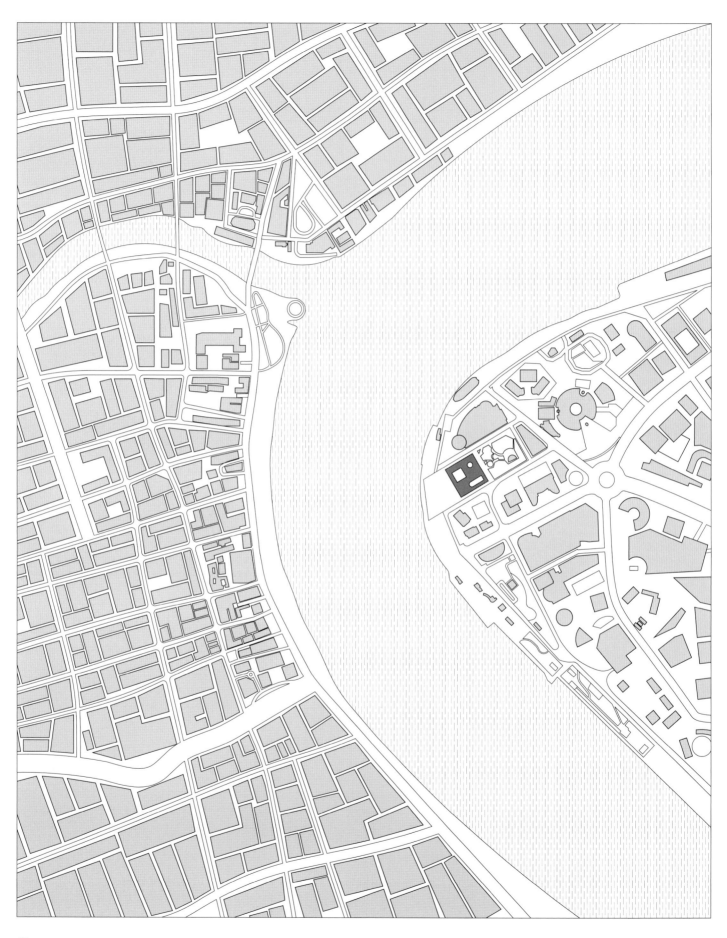

the future ruin
concept design for pudong art museum

Our proposal for the Pudong Art Museum is embodied by three architectural elements we have conceived of as enduring relics. We envision these 'urban artefacts' as constants that are able to endure for decades and perhaps even millennia, and which can be adapted for various functions beyond the life of the museum itself. The central design concept is informed by the Chinese notion of 'ruin' as an embodiment of both temporal continuity and loss and absence. Although the site and programme both call for a monumental architecture, our definition of the monument goes beyond superficial image-making: Pudong does not need another shape to add to its skyline; what it needs is an icon that can represent both the history and the future of the city, which is able to withstand the test of time.

The archetypal geometries used in our design – arch, square and circle, representing Earth, Heaven and Gateway respectively – are timeless motifs dating back to ancient Chinese cosmology. Conceived as stand-alone spatial totems and cores, each of them contains a unique vertical circulation connected to various functions clustered around its periphery. The Earth zone houses artist studios and spaces for art production, while the Heaven zone is a library contained within a circular core surrounded by classrooms and educational facilities. The Gateway atrium, framed by 40 m (131 ft)-high walls, is a naturally lit void, tied together by suspended bridges between different levels. Surrounding this atrium is a series of white-box gallery spaces. An orchestrated journey encourages visitors to circulate via the bridges, purposefully interrupting the monotonous experience of visiting a conventional art gallery. Like a cleansing of the palate, this circulation assures that visitors visually reset between galleries.

The exterior of the building features a pronounced urban gesture of a continuous, raised public plinth, which extends across to a waterfront park. The plinth, with its various geometric sunken courtyards for sculpture viewing and gathering, implies an imagined archaeological ground serving as the foundation for the three spatial totems. Rather than creating a monument that aspires to be an image of finality and urban spectacle, we pursue the less explored path of an architecture whose iconicity invites change and the forces of evolution, weathering and perpetual transformation.

shanghai

competition

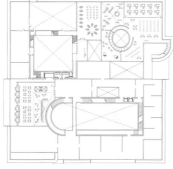

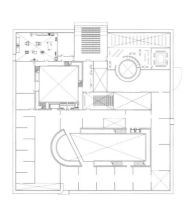

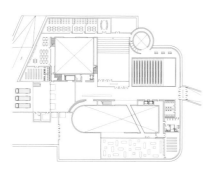

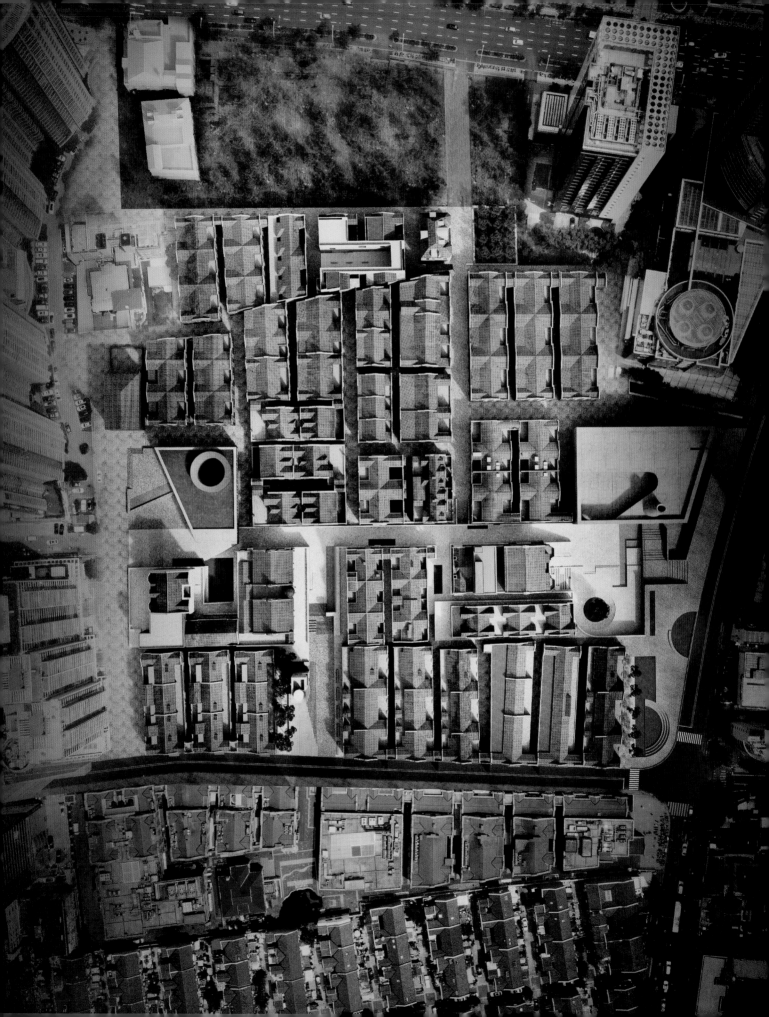

cultural arcadia
zhang yuan competition

In the midst of the ever-evolving metropolis of Shanghai, there is a growing nostalgia for its past. The Zhang Yuan site, historically defined by its communal functions, used to bring a sense of urban connectivity. Built by a British merchant in the late 1870s and later sold to a businessman as a private garden, it was famed for its entertainment and urban cultural diversions. Over recent years, although Zhang Yuan has fallen into dilapidation, it is largely recognized as Shanghai's largest and most intact *longtang* (lane house) compound. And, like many other *longtang* relics, Zhang Yuan remains relevant for its symbolic link to the intimate streetscape that defines the very essence of Shanghai living. In order to continue Shanghai's unique lineage, we have deployed a series of careful interventions based on the concept of 'cultural arcadia', instead of insisting on a precise reconstruction of the past.

At the main entries at the four cardinal points, newly planned structures correspond to the historical functions of Zhang Yuan, turning the entire complex into an icon as well as creating connections back to the city. We insert four elements – the Forum (an event space), the Tower (an observation tower), the Stage (a performance centre), and the House (a boutique hotel). The Forum consists of a floating geometric volume and a circular, cavernous space located at the centre of the site, hovering over the sunken plaza to serve as the landmark for the entry. The Stage greets visitors at the southern entrance off the main urban road. The Tower, a vertical landmark located on the west side next to the internal promenade, allows visitors to capture a bird's-eye view of the entire complex. Finally, the House, a boutique hotel that integrates the old and the new architecture, is located at the east entrance. With the excavation of the original ground, an inserted landscape is established to allow the historic *shikumen* architecture of Zhang Yuan to be displayed like an urban artefact and celebrated as the cultural centre of the complex.

Today's Zhang Yuan continues to support a lively community despite the encroachment of modern commercial developments. The *longtang* as embodied by Zhang Yuan is more than just the charming architectural shell of the past; it represents a way of life now lost to us. What we aspire to preserve is not only the storied structures of a timeless community but also, and more importantly, the dynamism and collective lifestyle that the Zhang Yuan garden used to foster within its *longtang* neighbourhoods.

shanghai

competition

1

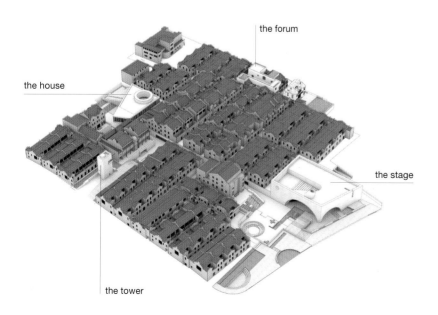

the forum

the house

the stage

the tower

2

3

4

1 forum view 2 the tower 3 sunken piazza and tower 4 the stage   **future artefact .** cultural arcadia 313

the vertical city
civic centre in zhengzhou

For Yuhua Civic Centre located in western Zhengzhou, our ambition is to design an iconic landmark for the city, which celebrates the region's history and culture while simultaneously projecting its own future lineage that can outlast the fleeting trends of today. Since the typology of the civic centre should be unquestionably fit to serve the community, it is essential that we create a monument for the city that is connected to its cultural roots as they hold special significance to the local citizens. Taking cues from the region's vernacular heritage of cave dwellings, or *yaodong*, we propose an urban artefact that recalls the primitive, primordial and even instinctive act of construction for an iconic monument, based on the notion of objecthood combined with the act of excavation as the main design language.

The Civic Centre floats as a cube with 38 m (125 ft)-long sides above an open plaza; here we are referencing the architect Louis Kahn, who regarded the square as an element notable for its simple yet assertive presence, carrying both modern and timeless characteristics. The overall massing conforms to the cube, with façades adopting a faceted, chiselled profile. The use of coarse red brick is a gesture to return to the raw authenticity of vernacular building materials, a conscious shift away from the glass-and-steel structures that have taken over Zhengzhou's skyline in recent years. Starting from this strong archetypal formal approach, we slowly begin to interrogate its architectural 'body' from within. Different setback depths along the façades introduce complex textures to reflect the complexity of the cityscape, and reveal the public nature of the internal programmes.

Looking up from the centre of the sunken courtyard, where the lobby and exhibition hall are located, the visitor gains a theatrical spatial experience of seeing a giant cube floating above. The centre of the boulder-like cube is excavated to form three interlinking atriums, open towards the sky. Introducing light within livens up the interior, and thus light becomes an element that shapes the interior experience. All the main functions are organized around the voids, evoking stone caves of different sizes and connected by bridges.

There are two journeys designed for visitors. One is an ascending spiral ramp that surrounds the three atriums, allowing the visitor to perceive changes in lighting and the relationship between the many interpenetrating perspectives offered by the sectional caves. The other path is a journey intentionally designed for all the major functions of the Civic Centre, charting an experience of the entire structure by passing through different geometrical spaces. Depending on the visitor's approach, the building can be read as a singular element or as one that is fractured but woven together again with fine details. The 'monument' achieved at the end is a nuanced celebration of the struggle between the pressures of the interior and the exterior, a form that invites plural readings and aspires to become an icon that serves as the backdrop for new collective memories in the city.

zhengzhou

architecture
interior

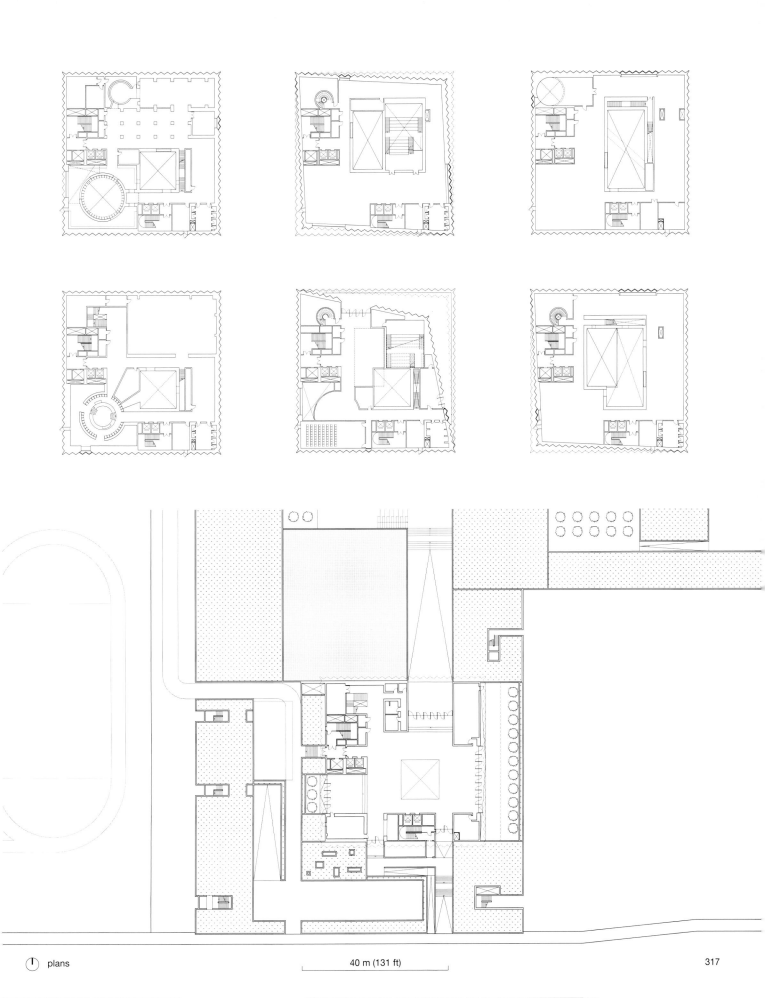

40 m (131 ft)

1

2

3

the forest
zhengzhou headquarters

1

Arriving at the *tabula rasa* project site in the rapidly expanding city of Zhengzhou, the confrontation between heritage and modernity is striking. Historically, the Central Plain area, in which the dynastic city first gained prominence by the end of the sixth century CE, was the cradle of ancient Chinese civilization. Zhengzhou today, as a fast-rising political and economic powerhouse, is in relentless pursuit of reinventing itself in the image of the future. Ancient monuments in the region, such as the city walls and fortress towers, often reveal a close relationship to the land in their built forms and construction materials. The current city plan charts new urban centres and also gestures towards the sky with clusters of glass towers, whose lightness, transparency and self-reflection proudly declare their existence as signs of modernity. For the commission to design a city block-sized, multi-use project in the midst of Zhengzhou in search of a new identity, we envision a forward-looking edifice that could coexist in harmony with layers of history, as well as being a vibrant present where new collective memories can be created.

The project is conceived as a forest, which allows for a sense of wholeness among heterogeneous parts of this project. Consisting of three separate buildings, the project creates outdoor and indoor public amenities to provide a lively social environment throughout the expansive grounds for the occupants. The gently curved roof profile softens the severity of the new district's zoning code, and hints at a contemporary interpretation of the eave forms deriving from the watchtowers of the historic city fortress.

The building's sense of permanence is imparted by the aggregation of structural elements. Comprising over 1,600 load-bearing arch walls, the project is an open system receptive to a range of indoor and outdoor functions. The individual bays, measuring 9 × 9 m (30 × 30 ft), can be flexibly configured according to a range of requirements. In the office component of the project, for example, the open floor plans provide large expanses to accommodate workstations, whereas private offices, meeting rooms and storage spaces occupy half or quarter of a bay. In public areas, such as the arrival lobby and sky-lit atriums, these structural bays are vertically stacked to celebrate collective gatherings.

Extending the rhythmic and adaptable logic outward, the façade is similarly considered as a space where the realms of the interior and exterior overlap, rather than a mere skin. The southern face of the building is punctured by either 4.5 m (15 ft)- or 9 m (30 ft)-deep verdant terraces, specifically designed for the use of office workers, as private residences, or for public functions. Intermittent glazing setbacks allow the hanging gardens to break up the scale of an otherwise brutal street wall, while also providing a sense of openness on the façade.

zhengzhou

architecture
masterplan
interior
products
environmental graphics

1 construction mock-up

2

Working in tandem with the massing articulation, the ground is sculpted to provide a varied landscape of seating, planters, reflecting pools and gardens. The sectional qualities and localized detailing suggest a sense of the past revealing itself. Bush-hammered stone blocks, terrazzo, vegetation and water elements hint at a weathered environment where nature and artifice become one. The history referenced here is not one of the dead and gone, nor a literal invocation of memories. Rather, we posit a particularly durable form of architecture, with the co-existence of the past and present as an active, open-ended, archaeological process, within which a new kind of contemporary life is possible.

Throughout the day, the play of light and shadow highlights the three-dimensional qualities of the concrete arches and the spaces within. Rigorous repetition of the structural members extends from the exterior hanging gardens, ground-level arcades and sunken courtyards to all interior grand lobbies, atriums and event spaces, creating a seamless integration of structure and space throughout. At times, the ambiguity is intentionally compounded, where nature is born out of artifice, and the manmade is embedded in the unrefined. The potentiality of the past resides in a utopic present, and the fleeting, visceral 'now' finds home in the ruin-like ground.

3

4

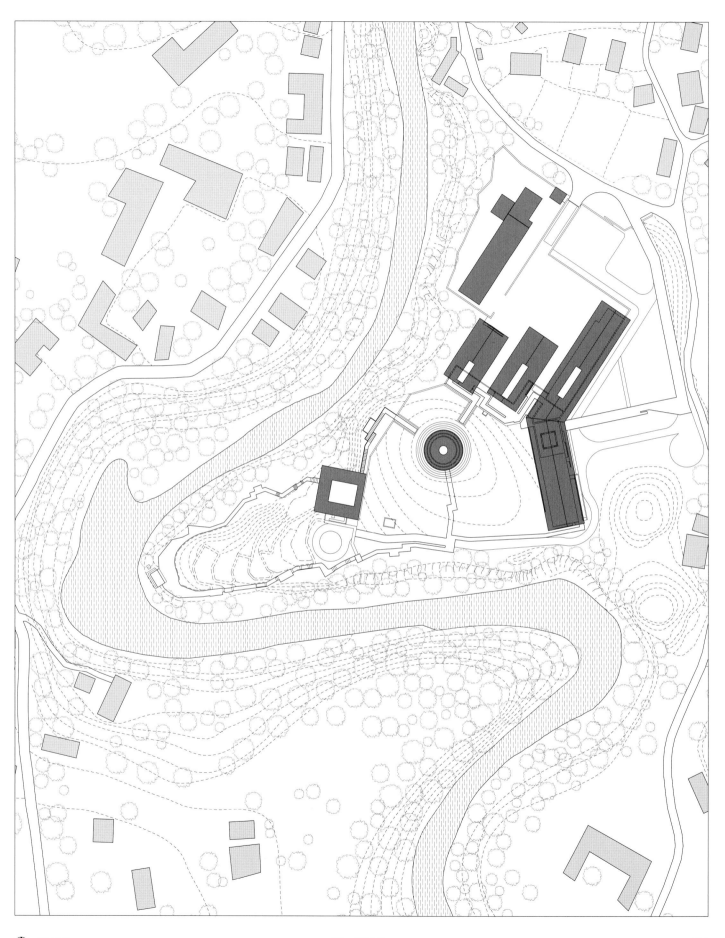

shan-shui: a duality
emeishan whisky distillery

For more than a thousand years Mount Emei has persisted as one of the most deeply spiritual places in China, being named a UNESCO World Heritage Site in 1996. The revered ground upon which our site sits has a rich history itself – through the centuries, this land was once an impressive monastery, the site of several historic battles, and a stopping point along many pilgrimage and trade routes. While any built remnants of the past no longer remain on site, its very emptiness is powerfully suggestive of all of its fabled memories. In this context, we were given the challenge of designing a distillery and home for China's first whisky, an opportunity to create a timeless architecture that speaks to the core values of a vision as well as the material and cultural heritage it aspires to sustain.

Surrounded on three sides by a winding creek, and with the majestic Emei peak as a backdrop, the site for this project is an exemplification of the Chinese notion of the duality of natural elements that make up the world we live in. *Shan-shui* literally means 'mountain-water.' While *shan* represents strength and permanence, *shui* represents fluidity and transformation; they are two opposing yet complementary forces. In the spirit of this philosophy, the position of the proposal is to conceive a gesture whose very strength lies in its humbleness and simplicity, with its profound respect for nature. When the two individual concepts combine, they produce a new layer of meaning that functions with new logics in another dimension. This paradigm is also manifested in the *shan-shui* painting, one of the three genres of traditional Chinese painting, in which the integration of two elements leads to a whole new level of the picturesque. The architecture offers a balanced duality in many ways, with the industrial buildings as a modern interpretation of vernacular Chinese architecture, and the visitor buildings as elemental geometries grounded in the terrain.

Three long buildings housing the whisky production facilities are situated at the north side of the site; parallel in formation, they are tucked into the gentle natural slope of the land with gradually descending rooflines. In an interpretation of vernacular architecture, reclaimed clay tiles give a humble texture to the pitched roofs that rest upon a modern concrete post-and-beam structure. The infill of rock walls is made from the boulders extracted from the ground during site levelling, so that the cycle of destruction and recreation may continue in permanent evolution.

emeishan

architecture
masterplan
interior
products
branding
environmental graphics

1

In contrast to the vernacular roots of the industrial buildings, the two visitor experience buildings are built upon fundamental geometries: the circle and the square. The round tasting-experience building is partially submerged in the ground, with five subterranean tasting rooms surrounding a domed courtyard that contains a cascading water feature in the middle. The upper part of the dome reveals itself out of the ground slightly; with three concentric brick rings perched atop, it subtly mirrors the silhouette of Mount Emei. This sculptural landform becomes an iconic presence that can be seen from every part of site, and meanwhile acts as a culminating destination from which visitors can enjoy a full panoramic vista. The square restaurant and bar building is located further down the topography, cantilevered on two sides with one corner hovering over the river bank. While the dining space is organized along the building's perimeter for open views, at the core an open-air courtyard is oriented to frame the Emei peak as a borrowed scene.

Besides revealing a deep appreciation for the site's natural resources, the project is also an embodiment of the refined sense of artistry embedded in whisky-making and blending, which is in dialogue with traditional Chinese craftsmanship and knowledge of materials. A variety of concrete, cement and stone mixtures forms the base material palette, finding resonance in the strong mineral presence of the site. Accent materials are drawn from those used in whisky craft, from the copper distillation pots to the aged oak casks. Throughout the project, we try to embody the Chinese concept of the dichotomy of two elements that exist in opposition yet complement each other, and to strike a harmonious balance between architecture and landscape, industry and visitor experience, mountain and water.

3

4

objects

For this final chapter, we have dedicated a space to highlight one of the key pillars of our practice, which was in large part founded in the early years on the making of design objects. Our work, in its totality, represents an interdisciplinary approach that seeks to find meaningful dialogue between furniture, accessories, product design and graphic design within architecture. 'Interdisciplinary' is often recast as a new buzzword or trend in the design profession, but the basic tenets were established by the Bauhaus and Art Nouveau movements. One forgets that although often associated too quickly with a particular 'style', these movements represented a larger collective ambition – a total design vision through means of controlling built environments from the large gestalt down to the smallest details. Mark Wigley, in his essay 'Whatever Happened to Total Design?' (1998), describes the duality and opposing impulses in exerting this control – one that is an implosion towards the interior, ultimately producing hyper-interiors, and the other as an expansion outwards into the urban sphere, creating a continuous interior. Part of Wigley's argument is that the nature of design produces totalizing environments: whether you produce a neutral white box or sculptural forms, the end effect is totalizing. Design is never neutral.

Turkish writer Orhan Pamuk published his novel *Museum of Innocence* in 2008; events took a curious turn when, in 2012, a real, bricks-and-mortar Museum of Innocence opened to visitors, housing a painstakingly curated collection of the objects described in the novel, amassed over decades by the author himself. Though the items are mostly commonplace – worn shoes, cigarette butts, a doorknob – their significance becomes elevated thanks to their intertwinement with the fictional narrative. In our own lives, we are constantly surrounded by objects, mostly mundane, but often containing significance or meaning for us. Perhaps you love the weight of an object in your hand, perhaps you cherish the memory that it recalls, or perhaps you respect the craft with which it was made. Our relationship to objects, our experience with them, is at once cognitive, emotive and physical.

Architectural objects, if we consider Vitruvian ideals, have been judged by the trifecta of beauty, structural integrity and utility. Or they can be, and often are in contemporary contexts, judged purely by their outward image. We recognize the inevitability of the discussion of form when it comes to architecture – we are not in denial of that aspect, but we seek form that is layered and complex, multidimensional, that cannot be reduced to a singular image. We aim for the objects we create to have the emotional, intellectual and physical impact on our being that the other objects we cherish naturally possess. As a result, at first glance, the architecture often appears obscure, or brutal, or even banal. Its potency is revealed only when effort is made, time is spent – through narrative, space, light, materiality and details. That is when its beauty begins to come forth.

1 nh1217 Collection . **Artemide**

2 Extend Mirrors . **De La Espada**

3 Yanzi . **Artemide**

4 Ming Chair . **Stellar Works**

5 Shaker Collection . **De La Espada**

6 The Society Collection . **Paola C**

7 Lianou Stool . **De La Espada**

8 Bai Family . **Parachilna**

9 Stay Collection . **Cassina**

10 Discipline Sofa . **Stellar Works**

11 One Child Policy . **Dollhouse of the Future**

12 B Bowl Basket . **She's Mercedes**

13 Cradle Sofa . **Arflex**

14 Shan Shui . **Neri&Hu**

15 Utility Chair . **Stellar Works**

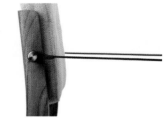

16 Capo Collection . De La Espada

17 Piasa Limited Edition . **Neri&Hu**

18 The Emperor Light . **Moooi**

19 Sedan Lounge Chair / Lantern Light . ClassiCon

20 Jian Collection . Gandia Blasco

21 Sul Sole Va Series . **Viabizzuno**

22 People Series . **Neri&Hu**

23 Together Chair . Fritz Hansen

24 Zisha . **Neri&Hu**

25 Xi Light . Poltrona Frau

26 Lan . Gan

27 Supporting Ren Collection . **Poltrona Frau**

28 Industry Chair . **Stellar Works**

29 Supporting Ren Collection . **Poltrona Frau**

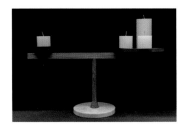

30 Balance . **Driade**

31 Common Comrades . **Moooi**

32 Immersion Tub . **Agape**

33 Cabinet of Curiosity . **Stellar Works**

34 Hanger . **Offecct**

35 Concrete Tile Shui . **LCDA**

36 Boli . **Neri&Hu**

37 Signs and Symbols . **Kanjian**

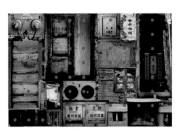

38 Remnant Carpet . **Moooi**

39 Eames Elephant . **Vitra**

40 Denglong Family . **Parachilna**

41 Wild Feast Picnic Basket .
Wallpaper* Handmade Sponsored
by Jaguar

42 Zodiac Puzzle . **Neri&Hu**

43 Solo Chair / Structure Table . **De La Espada**
Lacquer . **Neri&Hu**

44 Zisha . **When Objects Work**

45 The Narcissist . **BD Barcelona**

46 April Chair . **La Manufacture**

47 Commune Bench . **De La Espada**

48 USB . **Offecct**

49 Jie . **Nanimarquina**

50 Zhuang Box . **Poltrona Frau**

51 nh1217 Light . **Artemide**

project credits

black box redux [16–27]
number 31
Location: Shanghai
Date: 2018–2020
Client: Shanghai Jing Gong Group / China Postal &
   Telecommunications Appliances (East China)
Partners-in-charge: Lyndon Neri, Rossana Hu
Associate director-in-charge: Nellie Yang
Senior associate-in-charge: Federico Saralvo
Design team: Peng Guo, Yinan Li, Nicolas Fardet,
   Lili Cheng, Haiou Xin, Jacqueline Yam

the garage [28–39]
beijing b+ automobile service centre
Location: Beijing
Date: 2014–2016
Client: Wonderoll Auto Service Co Ltd
Partners-in-charge: Lyndon Neri, Rossana Hu
Senior associate-in-charge: Nellie Yang
Design team: Peng Guo, Begoña Sebastián,
   Lina Lee, Chris Yuan, Nicolas Fardet, Lili Cheng,
   Christine Neri, Siwei Ren, Haiou Xin

the unifying wall [40–9]
yuyuan road and together restaurant
Location: Shanghai
Date: 2015–2017
Client: Shanghai Creater Industrial Co Ltd
Yuyuan Road:
Partners-in-charge: Lyndon Neri, Rossana Hu
Associate-in-charge: Tony Schonhardt
Design team: Ouyang Jianqiu, Yinan Li, Christine Neri,
   Haiou Xin
Together Restaurant:
Partners-in-charge: Lyndon Neri, Rossana Hu
Senior associate-in-charge: Aleksandra Duka
Design team: Yinan Li, Mark Zhang, Siyu Chen,
   Sophia Wu, Nicolas Fardet, Simin Qiu, Haiou Xin,
   Jacqueline Yam

the convenience store [50–5]
little b retail concept
Location: Shanghai
Date: 2017
Client: Little B, The Beast
Partners-in-charge: Lyndon Neri, Rossana Hu
Associate-in-charge: Nellie Yang
Design team: Peng Guo, Susana Sanglas, Utsav Jain,
   Nicolas Fardet, Christine Neri, Haiou Xin

the recontextualization of history [56–79]
design commune and commune social
Location: Shanghai
Date: 2010–2012
Client: Design Republic, Inc
Partners-in-charge: Lyndon Neri, Rossana Hu

Associate-in-charge: Chunyan Cai
Design team: Jane Wang, Karen Fu, Peng Guo,
   Peter Eland, Jonas Hultman, Markus Stoecklein,
   Christina Cho, Jeongyon Mimi Kim, Ella Ye Lu,
   Federico Saralvo, Lei Zhao, Lei Xiao, Darcy Tang,
   Brian Lo, Yun Zhao, Nicolas Fardet, Xiaowen Chen,
   Christine Neri, Hao Zhou, Siwei Ren, Evelyn Chiu,
   Ivo Toplak

the vertical lane house [80–109]
waterhouse at south bund
Location: Shanghai
Date: 2008–2010
Client: Unlisted Collection Group
Waterhouse at South Bund:
Partners-in-charge: Lyndon Neri, Rossana Hu
Associate-in-charge: Debby Haepers
Design team: Chunyan Cai, Markus Stoecklein,
   Carmen Lee, Jane Wang, Brian Lo, Yun Zhao,
   Zhili Liu, Christine Neri, Vivi Lau
Table No.1 by Jason Atherton:
Partners-in-charge: Lyndon Neri, Rossana Hu
Director-in-charge: Dirk Weiblen
Design team: Briar Hickling, Jacqueline Min,
   Qixiao Feng, Daisy Yuan, Nicolas Fardet,
   Jean-Philippe Bonzon, Siwei Park

the unfolding village [112–15]
installation design for stockholm furniture &
   light fair 2019
Location: Stockholm
Date: 2018
Client: Stockholm Furniture & Light Fair
Partners-in-charge: Lyndon Neri, Rossana Hu
Senior associate-in-charge: Christine Chang
Design team: Kevin Chim, Malgorzata Mutkowska,
   Cheng Jia, Chengju Chang

the extroverted privacy [116–21]
wu residence
Location: Singapore
Date: 2009–2011
Client: Private owner
Partners-in-charge: Lyndon Neri, Rossana Hu
Associate-in-charge: Chunyan Cai
Design team: Jane Wang, Qi Liu, Andrew Roman

curio stair of encounters [122–7]
bloomberg hong kong office
Location: Hong Kong
Date: 2014–2015
Client: Bloomberg LP
Partners-in-charge: Lyndon Neri, Rossana Hu
Associate-in-charge: Christine Chang, Wendy Tsai
Design team: Dong Wu, Jiameng Li, Xuezhu Tian,
   Brian Lo, Yun Zhao, Christine Neri, Haiou Xin

the archives [128–33]
le méridien zhengzhou
Location: Zhengzhou
Date: 2009–2013
Client: Central China Real Estate Ltd
Partners-in-charge: Lyndon Neri, Rossana Hu
Associate-in-charge: Christina Luk
Design team: Lina Lee, Louise Ma, Jacqueline Min,
    Peter Eland, Alex Mok, Victor Ung, Eva Wieland,
    Zara Wang, Andrew Roman, Windy Zhang,
    Ni Duan, Meng Gong, Amy Hu, Begoña Sebastian,
    Anne Mu, Erika Lanselle, Debby Haepers,
    Chunyan Cai, Dagmar Niecke, Brian Lo, Yun Zhao,
    Jean-Philippe Bonzon, Xiaowen Chen, Nicolas
    Fardet, Ximi Li, Christine Neri, Siwei Ren, Evelyn
    Chiu, Litien Poeng, Hao Zhou

the muted landscape [134–9]
the sukhothai shanghai
Location: Shanghai
Date: 2013–2018
Client: HKR International Ltd
Partners-in-charge: Lyndon Neri, Rossana Hu
Senior associate-in-charge: Laurent Tek
Design team: Chloe Chiu, Akrawit Yanpaisan,
    Cao Fang, Daisy Yuan, Gail Chen, Jia Gu,
    Jiameng Li, Joanne Feng, Lara De Pedro,
    Megan Shen, Tracy Fong, Brian Lo, Mona He,
    Xiaowen Chen, Yun Zhao, Christine Neri,
    Litien Poeng, Siwei Ren, Chengju Chang

rethinking the split house [140–51]
private residence in tianzifang
Location: Shanghai
Date: 2011–2012
Client: Private owner
Partners-in-charge: Lyndon Neri, Rossana Hu
Associate-in-charge: Tony Schonhardt
Design team: Lei Xiao, Lei Zhao, Peng Guo

constellation of enclosures [154–9]
jisifang boutique
Location: Shanghai
Date: 2018
Client: Jisifang Co Ltd
Partners-in-charge: Lyndon Neri, Rossana Hu
Senior associate-in-charge: Federico Saralvo
Design team: Ivy Feng, Brendan Kellogg,
    Callum Holgate, Nicolas Fardet

the attic [160–3]
flamingo shanghai office
Location: Shanghai
Date: 2013–2014
Client: Flamingo Group
Partners-in-charge: Lyndon Neri, Rossana Hu
Associate-in-charge: Nellie Yang

Design team: Peng Guo, Begoña Sebastián,
    Anqing Zhu, Kelvin Huang, Brian Lo, Yun Zhao,
    Litien Poeng

the urban oasis [164–9]
alila bangsar
Location: Kuala Lumpur
Date: 2015–2018
Client: Keystone Land Development Sdn Bhd
Partners-in-charge: Lyndon Neri, Rossana Hu
Senior associate-in-charge: Federico Saralvo
Design team: Jacqueline Min, Briar Hickling,
    Xiaofeng Qi, Carmen Marin, Chiara Aliverti,
    Suju Kim, Daisy Yuen, Qi Liu, Nicolas Fardet,
    Lili Cheng, Litien Poeng

the covered hearth [170–3]
chi-q at three on the bund
Location: Shanghai
Date: 2013–2014
Client: Three on the Bund
Partners-in-charge: Lyndon Neri, Rossana Hu
Senior associate-in-charge: Laurent Tek
Design team: Jinlin Zheng, João Gonçalo Lopes,
    Brian Lo, Yun Zhao, Xiaowen Chen, Christine Neri,
    Siwei Park, Evelyn Chiu

the urban sanctum [174–83]
kimpton da an hotel
Location: Taipei
Date: 2017–2019
Client: Cornerstone Partners Group
Partners-in-charge: Lyndon Neri, Rossana Hu
Senior associate director-in-charge: Laurent Tek
Associate-in-charge: Chloe Chiu
Design team: Akrawit Yanpaisan, Federico Salmaso,
    James Beadnall, Chao Ji, Lara De Pedro,
    Christine Chang, Yannick Lo, Brian Lo,
    Junho Jeon, Mona He, Xiaowen Chen, Haiou Xin,
    Chengju Chang, Jacqueline Yam

the house of remembrance [184–7]
singapore residence
Location: Singapore
Date: 2017–ongoing
Client: Private owner
Partners-in-charge: Lyndon Neri, Rossana Hu
Senior associate-in-charge: Christine Chang
Design team: Sela Lim, Kevin Chim, Bella Lin

100 etchings: a journey within [190–3]
14th venice biennale 2014
Date: 2014
Organizer: Venice Biennale 2014
Partners-in-charge: Lyndon Neri, Rossana Hu
Senior associate-in-charge: Aleksandra Duka
Design team: Dan Xu, Nellie Yang

Design team: Valentina Brunetti, Fong Win Huang,
    Sela Lim, Lei Zhao, Callum Holgate, Leyue Chen,
    Sean Shen, Xin Liu, Bin Zhu, Nicolas Fardet,
    Yun Wang, Jin Zhang, Christine Neri, Haiou Xin

the void [288–305]
aranya art centre
Location: Qinhuangdao
Date: 2016–2019
Client: Aranya Real Estate Development Co Ltd
Partners-in-charge: Lyndon Neri, Rossana Hu
Associate director-in-charge: Nellie Yang
Design team: Ellen Chen, Peng Guo, Utsav Jain,
    Josh Murphy, Gianpaolo Taglietti, Zoe Gao,
    Susana Sanglas, Brian Lo, Lili Cheng

the future ruin [306–9]
concept design for pudong art museum
Location: Shanghai
Date: 2015–2016
Client: Shanghai Lujiazui Development
    (Group) Co Ltd
Partners-in-charge: Lyndon Neri, Rossana Hu
Associate-in-charge: Nellie Yang, Christine Chang
Design team: Josh Murphy, Kevin Chim, Sheila Lin,
    Christine Neri, Litien Poeng

cultural arcadia [310–13]
zhang yuan competition
Location: Shanghai
Date: 2019
Client: Shanghai Jing'an Planning and Natural
    Resources Bureau, Shanghai Jing'an Property
    (Group) Co Ltd
Partners-in-charge: Lyndon Neri, Rossana Hu
Senior associate-in-charge: Ziyi Cao
Design team: Yinan Li, Malgorzata Mutkowska,
    Jorik Bais, Davis Butner

the vertical city [314–19]
civic centre in zhengzhou
Location: Zhengzhou
Date: 2018–2019
Client: Yuhua Group
Partners-in-charge: Lyndon Neri, Rossana Hu
Associate-in-charge: Ziyi Cao
Design team: Fong Win Huang, Jorik Bais, Yinan Li,
    Fergus Davis, Akrawit Yanpaisan, Danyan Jin,
    Tessie Wan, Paz Ma, Nicolas Fardet,
    Xiangyu Gao, Lisa Kong

the forest [320–3]
zhengzhou headquarters
Location: Zhengzhou
Date: 2017–ongoing
Client: Youwell Group
Partners-in-charge: Lyndon Neri, Rossana Hu
Senior associate-in-charge: Chris Chen
Design team: Christine Chang, Wang Dian,
    Hwajung Song, Andrew Irvin, Jia Cheng,
    Binxing Yang, Tsen Yeoh, Malgorzata Mutkowska,
    Bernardo Taliani, Qiucheng Li, Lara De Pedro,
    Andy Chen, Paz Ma, Yangyang Chen, Dio Su,
    Becky Zhang, Eric Gu, Erin Chen, Lisa Chen,
    Travis Yang, Kevin Xie, Eric Zhou, Lili Cheng,
    Haiou Xin, Luna Hong, Xiaotang Tang

shan-shui: a duality [324–31]
emeishan whisky distillery
Location: Emeishan
Date: 2018–ongoing
Client: Pernod Ricard Group
Partners-in-charge: Lyndon Neri, Rossana Hu
Associate director-in-charge: Nellie Yang
Design team: Peng Guo, Utsav Jain, Feng Wang,
    Alexandra Heijink, Fergus Davis, Josh Murphy,
    Rosie Tseng, Vivian Bao, Yota Takaira,
    Nicolas Fardet, Lili Cheng, Haiou Xin, July Huang

brand collaborators [332–7]
Date: 2006–2020
Agape, Alpi, Arflex, Artemide, BD Barcelona,
Cassina, ClassiCon, De La Espada, Driade,
Fritz Hansen, Gandia Blasco, Kan Jian,
La Manufacture, LCDA, Lema, Magis, Meritalia,
Molteni&C, Moooi, Mosaico, Nanimarquina, Offecct,
Paola C, Parachilna, Petit H by Hermes, Poltrona
Frau, Porro, Really, Ritzenhoff, Riva 1920, San
Pellegrino, She's Mercedes, Steinway & Sons, Stellar
Works, Sulwhasoo, Swarovski, Turn, Viabizzuno, Vitra,
Wallpaper* Handmade, When Objects Work

biographies

LYNDON NERI, ROSSANA HU

Lyndon Neri and Rossana Hu are the founding partners of Neri&Hu Design and Research Office. Whether through objects of intimate daily use or vessels of inhabitation, they seek an approach to design that draws from multiple disciplines to provide experiences that enrich contemporary life while still keeping a critical linkage to a collective history.

Alongside their design practice, Lyndon and Rossana are deeply committed to architectural education and have lectured across the globe in various universities and professional forums. Together, they were appointed as the John C. Portman Design Critic in Architecture at the Harvard Graduate School of Design in 2019, and received the distinguished Norman R. Foster Visiting Professor Chair at Yale School of Architecture in 2018. They have previously taught at the University of Hong Kong Faculty of Architecture. They co-authored and edited *Persistence of Vision: Shanghai Architects in Dialogue*, published by MCCM Creations in 2007.

Lyndon and Rossana were also founding partners, in 2006, of Design Republic in Shanghai, a design platform incorporating retail concept, design and cultural exhibitions, and education. In 2015, they were appointed as the creative directors of Stellar Works, an international furniture brand that honours and advances the spirit and heritage of Asian crafts and traditions. Lyndon has been a board member of Roll & Hill LLC in Brooklyn since 2010, and Rossana has served on the International Advisory Board of the Shanghai Symphony Orchestra since 2018.

Lyndon Neri
Lyndon Neri received his Master's degree in Architecture from Harvard University Graduate School of Design and a Bachelor of Arts in Architecture from the University of California, Berkeley.

Rossana Hu
Rossana Hu received a Master's degree in Architecture and Urban Planning from Princeton University and a Bachelor of Arts in Architecture from the University of California, Berkeley, with a minor in music.

lyndon neri and rossana hu's office

NERI&HU DESIGN AND RESEARCH OFFICE

Founded in 2004 by partners Lyndon Neri and Rossana Hu, Neri&Hu Design and Research Office is an interdisciplinary architectural design practice based in Shanghai. The practice's burgeoning global portfolio includes commissions ranging from master planning and architecture to interior design, installation, furniture, product, branding and graphic works. Currently working on projects in many countries, Neri&Hu is composed of multicultural staff who speak more than thirty different languages. The diversity of the team reinforces a core vision for the practice: to respond to a global worldview incorporating overlapping design disciplines for a new paradigm in architecture.

Neri&Hu's location is purposeful. With Shanghai considered a new global frontier, Neri&Hu is at the immediate centre of this contemporary chaos. The city's cultural, urban and historical contexts function as a point of departure for design inquiries that span across a wide spectrum of scales. Furthermore, Neri&Hu has expanded the conventional boundaries of practice to include complementary disciplines. A critical probing into the specificities of programme, site, function and history is essential to the creation of rigorous work. Based on research, Neri&Hu anchors its ethos on the dynamic interaction of experience, detail, material, form and light rather than conforming to a formulaic style.

Neri&Hu and its designs have been recognized by a number of prestigious international awards spanning the fields of architecture, interior, product design and graphic design: Madrid Design Festival Award (2020); Design for Asia Grand Award (2020); Blueprint Overall Award for Design (2019); PLAN Award (2018); Designer of the Year, Elle Deco International Design Awards (2017); Interior Designers of the Year, Iconic Awards (2017); INSIDE – World Festival of Interiors (2017); Designer of the Year, Elle Deco Japan Design Awards (2016); Dezeen Hotlist (2016); Designer of the Year, Maison & Objet Asia (2015); Designer of the Year, Wallpaper* (2014); Far Eastern Architectural Design Award (2014); US Interior Design Hall of Fame induction (2013); Architectural Review Emerging Architecture Award (2010); Red Dot Award in Communication for Manifesto (2010); Design Vanguard, Architectural Record (2009).

Neri&Hu has been widely published and has received recognitions internationally. Neri&Hu's first monograph, *Neri&Hu Design and Research Office: Works and Projects 2004–2014*, was published by Park Books in 2017.

collaborators

NERI&HU DESIGN AND RESEARCH OFFICE STAFF
CURRENT

Anna Bai, Bi Jingyi, Ziyi Cao, Christine Chang, Allen Chen, Amanda Chen, Andy Chen, Chris Chen, Ginger Chen, Martin Chen, Chen Siyu, Chen Yangyang, Cheng Ningxin, Da Wenbo, Jerry Del Fierro, Lara De Pedro, Aleksandra Duka, Federica Esposito, Nicolas Fardet, Ivy Feng, Dania Angela Flores, Alexander Goh, Peng Guo, Utsav Jain, Joy Han, Luna Hong, Alfie Huang, Fresnel Hu, Kathy Hu, Rossana Hu, Fong Win Huang, July Huang, Scott Hsu, Kate Hwang, Ji Chao, Jessica Jiang, Jin Danyan, Canning Kong, Lina Lee, Jan Lee, Wan-ru Lee, Echo Li, Loe Li, Li Guanlin, Li Qiucheng, Li Xianhua, Li Yinan, Sela Lim, Jully Liu, Kany Liu, Serein Liu, Yvonne Liu, Cage Lu, Lu Junxi, Paz Ma, Jacqueline Min, Lyndon Neri, Cassiel Pei, Kenneth Qiao, Rovi Qu, Federico Saralvo, Nikki Shen, Ren Yang Tan, Shu Tong, Sheng Yin, Vivienne Shi, Sun Yi, Ath Supornchai, Ambesh Suthar, Bernardo Taliani de Marchio, Yvonne Tan, Tang Xiaotang, Tian Hua, Laurent Tek, Tessie Wan, Wang Dian, Wang Feng, Wang Hongzhen, Wang Jian, Phil Wang, Wang Qianting, Wang Yuxuan, Wang Zhikang, Haiou Xin, Xu Jichuan, Sanif Xu, Echo Yan, Yang Bingxin, Michael Yang, Nellie Yang, Stan Yang, Yang Yanru, Yelena Yang, Akrawit Yanpaisan, Peter Ye, Sherry Ye, Chao-Fu Yeh, Yoki Yu, Andy Zhang, Alan Zhang, Becky Zhang, Helen Zhang, Weili Zhang, Lei Zhao

picture credits

notes

1   Svetlana Boym, 'Nostalgia', *Monumenttotransformation.Org*, 2011, monumenttotransformation.org/atlas-of-transformation/html/n/nostalgia/nostalgia-svetlana-boym.html. Accessed 25 April 2019.

2   Bin Qu, 'On Garden-Visiting and Scales', *C Foundation*, https://mp.weixin.qq.com/s/6M2O5wmp2qf3eFUoYo5mgw. Accessed 17 December 2020.

3   Ming Dong Gu, *Chinese Theories of Fiction* (Albany: State University of New York Press, 2006).

4   Gaston Bachelard and Maria Jolas (trans.), *The Poetics of Space* (1958; Boston: Beacon Press, 1994)

5   Martin Heidegger and Albert Hofstadter (trans.), *Poetry, Language, Thought* (1971; New York: Harper Perennial Modern Thought, 2013).

6   Paul Bowles, *The Sheltering Sky* (1949; New York: Ecco Press, 2014).

7   Gottfried Semper, *The Four Elements of Architecture and Other Writings* (1851; Cambridge: Cambridge University Press, 2011).

8   Beatriz Colomina, 'Intimacy and Spectacle: The Interiors of Adolf Loos', *AA Files* 20 (1990): 5–15, www.jstor.org/stable/29543700. Accessed 10 Dec 2020.

9   Jean La Marche, *The Familiar and the Unfamiliar in Twentieth-Century Architecture* (Urbana: University of Illinois Press, 2003).

10   Robert Venturi, *Complexity and Contradiction in Architecture* (New York: Museum of Modern Art, 1977).

11   Semper, *The Four Elements of Architecture*.

12   Jun'ichiro Tanizaki, *In Praise of Shadows* (1933; New Haven: Leete's Island Books, 1977). http://pdf-objects.com/files/In-Praise-of-Shadows-Junichiro-Tanizaki.pdf. Accessed 10 December 2020.

13   Richard Sennett, *Building and Dwelling: Ethics for the City* (London: Penguin Books, 2019).

14   Wu Hung, 'Shitao (1642–1707) and the Traditional Chinese Conception of Ruins', *Proceedings of the British Academy*, vol. 167, 2009 Lectures, pp.263–94.

15   Pierre Nora, 'Between Memory and History: Les Lieux de mémoire', *Representations* 26 (Spring 1989): 7–24.